Web 2.0

TECHNOLOGY 360

Web 2.0

Andrew A. Kling

LUCENT BOOKS
A part of Gale, Cengage Learning

GALE
CENGAGE Learning

Detroit • New York • San Francisco • New Haven, Conn • Waterville, Maine • London

LIBRARY OF CONGRESS CATALOGING-IN-PUBLICATION DATA

Kling, Andrew A., 1961-
    Web 2.0 / by Andrew A. Kling.
       p. cm. — (Technology 360)
    Includes bibliographical references and index.
    ISBN 978-1-4205-0171-1 (hardcover)
    1. Web 2.0.—Juvenile literature. 2. Online social networks—Juvenile literature. I. Title.
    TK5105.88817.K58 2010
    006.7'5—dc22
    2010028893

Lucent Books
27500 Drake Rd
Farmington Hills MI 48331

ISBN 13: 978-1-4205-0171-1
ISBN 10: 1-4205-0171-2

Printed in the United States of America
1 2 3 4 5 6 7 14 13 12 11 10

Printed by Bang Printing, Brainerd, MN, 1st Ptg., 12/2010

CONTENTS

"As we go forward, I hope we're going to continue to use technology to make really big differences in how people live and work."
—Sergey Brin, cofounder of Google

The past few decades have seen some amazing advances in technology. Many of these changes have had a direct and measurable impact on the way people live, work, and play. Communication tools, such as cell phones, satellites, and the Internet, allow people to keep in constant contact across longer distances and from the most remote places. In fields related to medicine, existing technologies—digital imaging devices, robotics, and lasers, for example—are being used to redefine surgical procedures and diagnostic techniques. As technology has become more complex, however, so have the related ethical, legal, and safety issues.

Psychologist B.F. Skinner once noted that "the real problem is not whether machines think but whether men do." Recent advances in technology have, in many cases, drastically changed the way people view the world around them. They can have a conversation with someone across the globe at lightning speed, access a huge universe of information with the click of a key, or become an avatar in a virtual world of their own making. While advances like these have been viewed as a great boon in some quarters, they have also opened the door to questions about whether or not the speed of technological advancement has come at an unspoken price. A closer examination of the evolution and use of these devices provides a deeper understanding of the social, cultural, and ethical implications that they may hold for our future.

Technology 360 not only explores how evolving technologies work, but also examines the short- and long-term impact of their use on society as a whole. Each volume in Technology 360 focuses on a particular invention, device, or family of similar devices, exploring how the device was developed; how it works; its impact on society; and possible future uses. Volumes also contain a time line specific to each topic, a glossary of technical terms used in the text, and a subject index. Sidebars, photos and detailed illustrations, tables, charts, and graphs help further illuminate the text.

Titles in this series emphasize inventions and devices familiar to most readers, such as robots, digital cameras, iPods, and video games. Not only will users get an easy-to-understand, "nuts and bolts" overview of these inventions, they will also learn just how much these devices have evolved. For example, in 1973 a Motorola cell phone weighed about 2 pounds (0.9 kg) and cost $4000.00—today, cell phones weigh only a few ounces and are inexpensive enough for every member of the family to have one. Lasers—long a staple of the industrial world—have become highly effective surgical tools, capable of reshaping the cornea of the eye and cleaning clogged arteries. Early video games were played on large machines in arcades; now, many families play games on sophisticated home systems that allow for multiple players and cross-location networking.

IMPORTANT DATES

1969

The first successful connection between computers is established when a computer at the University of California, Los Angeles (UCLA) communicates with a computer at Stanford University. The connection becomes the backbone of the ARPANET, the first computer communications network.

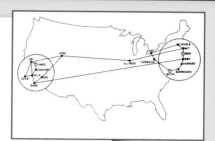

1993

Netscape's Mosaic, the first practical browser, debuts. There are fifty public servers on the World Wide Web.

1989– 1990

Tim Berners-Lee, a researcher at CERN in Geneva, Switzerland, proposes a facility-wide network based on hypertext linking, which he first calls "Mesh" and then later "World Wide Web."

1995

Secure socket layer protocols make online commercial transactions more secure. Amazon.com and eBay debut.

1970

1990

1970s– 1980s

The ARPANET expands to include research facilities and universities across the United States and connects to similar networks in Europe.

1991

The World Wide Web's first page debuts on CERN's network.

1994

There are more than fifteen hundred servers available on the World Wide Web. Netscape's Navigator browser debuts.

in the Development of Web 2.0

2001
Wikipedia debuts.

1998
Google debuts.

1999
Web designer Darcy DiNucci coins the phrase *Web 2.0*. Shawn Fanning revolutionizes music sharing with Napster.

2004
Thefacebook.com (later Facebook) debuts as a social network for Harvard University.

2007
Apple introduces the iPhone, which helps to popularize the concept of accessing the Internet on a cell phone.

2009
Actor Ashton Kutcher becomes the first Twitter user to have 1 million followers.

2006
Twitter debuts.

2000

2010

2002
Social network Friendster debuts and attracts 3 million users in its first six months of operation.

2005
YouTube debuts in a trial version.

2010
Facebook has more than 450 million users worldwide.

An Eighth Grader and the World Wide Web

Heather Coken is an eighth grader living in Rhode Island. The World Wide Web is a significant presence in her life. She uses it daily for a variety of purposes and chuckles when asked how often she uses it, saying, "I use it a lot."[1]

Heather explains how the Internet is part of her daily schoolwork. Most of her textbooks are online, such as her "social studies book, math book, and science book."[2] She discusses her homework assignments with her friends via text messages on her cell phone, or through instant messaging on her Google account.

Heather also talks about how much she uses the Web for entertainment. She and her friends watch music or funny videos on YouTube, and she mentions that she uses Web sites to research ticket prices for concerts. Her father adds that Heather also likes to use the Internet for shopping.

But Heather also understands that the Internet has much more to offer. So far, her parents have trusted her with some Web-based technologies, such as text messaging. She says that she is responsible enough with her texting use that "my dad doesn't tell me to get off the phone,"[3] but other aspects of the Web are off-limits right now. She says her mother "wants me to wait until high school"[4] to sign up for a social network, such as Facebook.

In these and many other ways, Heather is a typical teenager. There are limits to and rules concerning what she can do on the Internet. She takes full advantage of what is available to her and cannot wait until she is older in order to experience more of what the Web has to offer.

Many of Heather's experiences on the Internet are part of what is called Web 2.0 (pronounced "web two-oh"). The term is used to describe the interactive nature of today's Internet experience, in which millions of visitors to the Web can do much more than just look at a computer screen.

In just a few short years, the average Internet experience has moved from reactive to interactive. Today's Web 2.0 experience allows even the most casual users to provide feedback to what they see and hear online and, perhaps just as importantly, share what they have created with the Internet community. Web 2.0 offers photos, videos, music, and news, but users' opinions and feelings are also available with amazing speed and spontaneity. And it is available through an ever-expanding variety of devices, such as laptop or notebook computers and cellular phones. This increasing ease of access leads to debates of safety, privacy, and security by experts from such widely varying fields as education, finance, and copyright law. The Web 2.0 experience has revolutionized the Internet, and each new development in interaction makes it even more valuable to users of all ages.

CHAPTER 1

Web 1.0 Evolves into Web 2.0

Today's Internet experience allows computer users to view and interact with content from around the world. This concept of user-driven content as used and enjoyed by Heather Coken and millions like her is a far cry from the origins of the Internet. Its origins lie in the early days of computer research, when scientists around the world began to envision ways to use these machines to share their ideas and discoveries. Some went as far as to envision a day when nonscientists could use computers as well, to access the world's knowledge.

The First Computer Network

In the 1960s computers were being used for scientific research at a number of universities and companies in the United States and Europe. But the computers were unable to communicate with each other, and the scientists who used them had no means of sharing information electronically. With funding from the U.S. Department of Defense's Advanced Research Projects Agency (ARPA), American scientists began working on ways to link computers by sending data over telephone lines through a process

BITS & BYTES

4

Number of computers connected in the first network in 1969

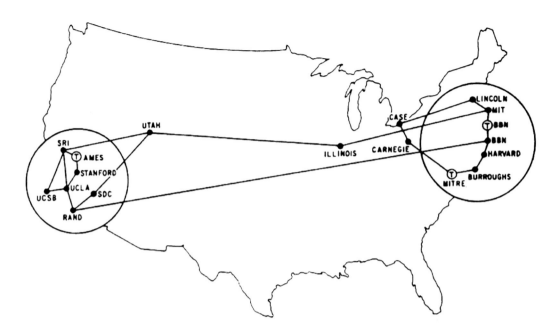

called packet switching. This technique breaks the data that comprises messages into smaller sizes, called "packets." This made data more easily transmittable along existing telephone lines.

ARPA's hope was to link computers at the nation's major defense operations in order to ensure communications in the case of the outbreak of nuclear war with the Soviet Union. ARPA provided monetary grants to leading scientists from both universities and engineering firms to advance computer science and to establish the first computer network among four computers. Three were in California, at Stanford University; the University of California, Santa Barbara; and the University of California, Los Angeles (UCLA); the fourth was in Utah at the University of Utah. These four comprised the ARPANET, the world's first computer network.

On October 29, 1969, Charley Kline, a student programmer at UCLA, sent the first message from one computer to another on the ARPANET along an existing telephone line. With his professor, Leonard Kleinrock, supervising, Kline attempted to connect his computer with the ARPANET computer at Stanford using the word *login*. However, the system crashed between the letters *o* and *g*, so, strictly

CONNECTING TO THE INTERNET

1 To connect to the Internet, a computer begins by sending out a message requesting a webpage. This message goes through a cable or phone line to a number of powerful computers, known as servers, owned by the user's Internet Service Provider (ISP).

Internet Service Provider

2 From there, the message is forwarded along to a Network Access Point (NAP). These connection points are located around the world, and make it possible for computer messages to travel from one network to another.

4 Messages encounter numerous computers known as routers, which direct the flow of internet traffic. By looking at the unique Internet Protocol (IP) addresses linked to a message, the router can identify what site the user is looking for, and direct messages and information accordingly. The receiving computer will interpret the original message, and send back the requested information – the web page.

3 Messages move from one NAP to another through a structure called an internet "backbone." These high speed cables are typically made of optical fiber (they are also known as fiber optic cables), which transmit information through light pulses sent along flexible glass or plastic fibers.

Despite the many steps involved, breakthroughs in cable and computer technology have made this complicated process astonishingly fast, allowing for the rapid information transfer that is essential for Web 2.0 applications.

speaking, the first message sent across the ARPANET was actually "lo." The crash occurred when memory allocated in the computer for the login operation was not made available for the operation. The crash was repaired within an hour after the Stanford machine was rebooted, and the message was resent successfully.

In some ways, accessing a computer in 1969 was similar to accessing a server today. Users sat at a keyboard at terminals that were connected to the main computer. According to Kleinrock, "what we were [trying to do] as far as the [Stanford] machine was concerned, was to log in as a local terminal . . . the [Stanford] operating system to which we were logging in had no notion that it was in a network, but simply that it had local terminals that wanted access, and we were one such local terminal"[5] that was actually approximately 400 miles (644 km) away. A permanent connection was created between the two computers on November 21 as the new networking software

The "Intergalactic Computer Group"

In 1962 the U.S. Department of Defense's Advanced Research Projects Agency (ARPA) hired J.C.R. Licklider, an early proponent of computer communications, to establish a computer network. Under his direction, about a dozen universities and companies worked on ARPA contracts across the United States. In a series of memos to his fellow researchers in 1963, Licklider jokingly addressed them as members of the "Intergalactic Computer Group."

The name revealed that Licklider believed that communication among computer systems was essential. With it, researchers could build upon each other's work, no matter where they were located. In other words, he was envisioning a network. He notes, "It will possibly turn out that only on rare occasions do most or all of the computers in the overall system operate together in an integrated network. It seems to me important, nevertheless, to develop a capability for integrated network operation."

Licklider left ARPA in 1964 before his network became a reality. But his dream endured as several members of his Intergalactic Computer Group continued to work toward what later became the ARPANET.

Quoted in Katie Hafner and Matthew Lyon, *Where Wizards Stay Up Late: The Origins of the Internet*, New York: Simon & Schuster, 1996, p. 38.

was further refined. This marked the debut of the first computer network; by December, the first four ARPANET computers were permanently connected.

E-mail Revolutionizes Communication

By 1971 the ARPANET had been up and running for more than a year. Researchers working on the same computer within the system were able to type basic messages to each other, and, according to historian Janet Abbate, "by mid-1971 . . . several ARPANET sites had begun experimenting with ideas for simple programs that would transfer a message from one computer to another and place it in a designated 'mailbox' file."[6]

At the same time, Ray Tomlinson, a programmer at the pioneering computing firm Bolt, Beranek and Newman, was working on how to send messages from a computer on one system to another computer on a different system. The first use of electronic mail, or e-mail, came in late 1971 when Tomlinson sent a message between two computers connected to the ARPANET that, in his words, "were literally side by side."[7] He tested the program by sending several test messages on the network to himself. Tomlinson recalls,

> The test messages were entirely forgettable and I have, therefore, forgotten them. Most likely the first message was QWERTYUIOP or something similar. When I was satisfied that the program seemed to work, I sent a message to the rest of my group explaining how to send messages over the network. The first use of network email announced its own existence.[8]

Tomlinson also created the use of the @ symbol to designate the host computer. To him, it made perfect sense. He says, "The purpose of the at sign (in English) was to indicate a unit price (for example, 10 items @ $1.95). I used the at sign to indicate that the user was 'at' some other host rather than being local."[9]

Tomlinson's innovation quickly became a success. By 1973, 75 percent of all traffic on the network was e-mail. Researchers used it to work with colleagues, system operators used it to log hardware and software problems, and supervisors used it to check in with employees. The *ARPANET Completion Report,* written in 1978, called e-mail "a smashing success" and predicted that it would "sweep the country."[10]

By 1978 the ARPANET was not alone. Other regional networks had been built in the United States, notably in Hawaii and in the San Francisco, California, area. Additionally, networks were constructed in Great Britain, France, and Norway, and a satellite-based network spanned the Atlantic Ocean. Each had different communications protocols; in other words, each used different methods for transmitting data. The result was that an ARPANET researcher at the Massachusetts Institute of Technology (MIT) in Cambridge, Massachusetts, was unable to communicate with a colleague in Paris, France, via computer. Researchers from the United States and Europe pondered how to link all of these computers into one network.

TCP/IP

The communication protocols breakthrough came in 1974. Robert Kahn, an ARPANET program manager, enlisted the aid of Vinton Cerf, a twenty-nine-year-old assistant professor at Stanford University, to address the problem. They had worked together in developing the first ARPANET installation at UCLA, and Cerf had been one of the first designers

Vinton Cerf (left) and Robert Kahn helped to revolutionize the early Internet by developing a system they called Transmission Control Protocol, or TCP, which ensured a seamless transition of packets from network to network.

of the network's protocols. Kahn and Cerf developed a system they called transmission control protocol (TCP), which ensured a seamless transition of packets from network to network. Cerf recalls, "We wanted to have a common protocol and a common address space so that you couldn't tell . . . that you were actually talking through all these different kinds of nets,"[11] because having different protocols would emphasize the differences between networks.

Kahn and Cerf also proposed the creation of "gateways," which were special computers connected to one or more networks through which all internetwork traffic would pass. The gateways would maintain addresses of each network and convert packet formats when necessary. This idea was later refined into "internetwork protocol" (later shortened to "Internet protocol," or IP). This system simply passed individual packets between machines, while TCP handled the task of ordering packets into reliable connections between hosts, or computers capable of computer connection.

In 1977 ARPA demonstrated the feasibility of the technology. Experimenters sent packets from the San Francisco network to an ARPANET gateway, then through the ARPANET to a satellite network gateway on the East Coast, via satellite to Europe, and back to California through the ARPANET. It was a success. Computer scientists across the networks recognized the value of TCP/IP, and over the next few years, implemented it whenever new computers joined the networks and converted all of their older systems to accommodate it.

The idea of an internetwork was becoming a reality. Additional networks sprang up around the United States and around the globe. In 1983 the Department of Defense split the original ARPANET into MILNET (for military use) and ARPANET (for civilian research sites). With university researchers now the dominant presence on the ARPANET, it took on a more civilian character. The National Science Foundation funded a network, called NSFNET, for colleges and universities that did not receive ARPA funding. The NSFNET went online in 1986 and connected to networks in Germany, Australia, Israel, Japan, and Finland. The internet

What Is TCP/IP?

The backbone of the Internet is the technology that enables one computer to communicate with another over a network. This technology is called TCP/IP. TCP stands for transmission control protocol, and IP stands for Internet protocol. A protocol is a method by which computers exchange information, via a telephone line, a satellite signal, or other means. TCP/IP was developed by Robert Kahn and Vinton Cerf in the 1970s and today remains the backbone of Web transmissions. Its success lies in its design, in which any network can communicate with any other, regardless of software or hardware configurations.

TCP/IP works in two parts: sending and receiving information. According to Katie Hafner, writing for the *New York Times*, Kahn and Cerf's breakthrough TCP

> defines a standard way to package chunks of data into "datagrams," for sending across the network. The Internet Protocol provides a standard way of putting those datagrams into envelopes addressed to any computer in the world. Like postal sorters, the computers along the way can look at the addresses on the envelopes to relay them to their destinations without needing to look inside the envelopes.

Katie Hafner, "Laurels for Giving the Internet Its Language," *New York Times*, February 16, 2005, www.nytimes.com/2005/02/16/technology/16internet.html.

work, or more simply, the "Internet" framework began to expand more rapidly than ever before.

Hypertext

By 1987 nearly thirty thousand hosts were connected to the Internet. ARPA decided to turn over control of its portion of the network to NSFNET, which had been built with more modern technology, such as higher-speed telephone lines and faster switching capabilities. The ARPANET was formally shut down in February 1990.

Researchers working on the various networks around the world often took advantage of an innovation called hypertext to create and share a variety of databases and manuals. Hypertext enabled writers to create shortcuts from one entry to another or to move between portions of a document; it was particularly valuable in help files and tables of contents.

One early application of hypertext occurred at Brown University in Providence, Rhode Island, where it was applied in an English literature course in the late 1980s. The course had a hypertext database with biographical sketches of the authors covered in the course, essays and discussions of styles and techniques, and portraits, drawings, and reproductions of works of art. This database was only accessible through the university's network and computers. No one outside the network could access the information. But this hypertext database and others like it eventually became the first pages on the World Wide Web, thanks to the vision of a British physicist who wanted to make accessing research data easier.

Tim Berners-Lee and the World Wide Web

At the same time that Brown students were becoming familiar with hypertext, Tim Berners-Lee, a British physicist and computer scientist, was working at the Swiss research facility Conseil Européen pour la Recherche Nucléaire (European Council for Nuclear Research) and was refining an idea for a network he first called "Mesh." The facility, commonly known as CERN, was, and is still today, a facility visited by physicists from around the world. They perform experiments with CERN's specialized equipment and then return to their university or company to analyze their collected data. Berners-Lee, then thirty-five years old, had spent his spare time for several years trying to create a records system that would allow all CERN researchers to access documents within the network, whether they were at the facility or not. He envisioned creating hypertext links for each document in CERN's database which would allow anyone with an Internet connection to access the information.

In 1989 Berners-Lee proposed his system to managers at CERN, who took no action on it. Little by little, Berners-Lee

enlisted aid from others at CERN and convinced them of the worth of his idea, which he was now calling the "World Wide Web."

In his book *Weaving the Web* Berners-Lee writes,
a person should be able to link with equal ease to any document wherever it happened to be stored . . . for the Web, the external link is what would allow it to actually become "worldwide." The important design element would be to ensure that when two groups had started to use the Web completely independently at different institutions, a person in one group could create a link to a document from the other with only a small incremental effort, and without having to merge the two document databases or even have access to the other system. If everyone on the Web could do this, then a single hypertext link could lead to an enormous, unbounded world.[12]

During a twentieth anniversary celebration of the World Wide Web, Tim Berners-Lee poses next to the computer he used to first run the World Wide Web while performing research at CERN.

Refining the Idea
and Revealing the Web

Despite the official inaction by CERN management, Berners-Lee continued to pursue his dream unofficially, in his spare time. By the following year, he had developed standards for hypertext markup language (HTML), which describes how to format pages containing hypertext links and created the code for hypertext transfer protocol (HTTP), the language computers would use to communicate over the World Wide Web. In addition, he formulated what at first was called the universal resource identifier, later known as the uniform resource locator (URL), which was the design for document addresses.

The World Wide Web debuted in 1991 with the first Web page posted on CERN's network. In a fashion similar to the first e-mail, the first Web page announced the Web's existence, explained its purpose, and how it could be used.

It is important to remember that at this point, the Internet was restricted to the scientific community, such as universities and research facilities, like CERN and the military. It is also important to understand that each user accessed the Internet based on the computer in use and where it was located. The hardware of many computers was able to view and follow links in hypertext-based documents through programs called browsers, but these browsers could only read hypertext documents that were located on the mainframe to which the computer was connected. However, Berners-Lee and his colleagues envisioned something grander. He writes,

> For an international hypertext system to be worthwhile ... many people would have to post information. The physicist would not find much information on quarks, nor the art student on Van Gogh, if many people and organizations did not make their information available in the first place. Not only that, but much information—from phone numbers to current ideas to today's menu—is constantly changing, and is only as good as it is up-to-date. That meant that anyone (authorized) should be able to publish and correct

The World's First Webcam

Today Webcams provide a multitude of information. They can display weather conditions around the world, traffic congestion, and nature's wonders, like the eruption of Yellowstone National Park's Old Faithful geyser. But the first Webcam recorded a much more mundane activity.

In 1991 students in the computing laboratory at England's Cambridge University decided that they were wasting precious time by leaving their computers to go to the lounge to check the coffee pot to see if the coffee had finished brewing or if the pot needed refilling. So they set up a camera that focused on the coffee-maker and connected it to their internal network. The camera was connected to the Internet in 1993 and became a popular destination for early Web surfers. The camera was shut off for the last time in 2001 and the last coffeemaker used in the lab was auctioned off on eBay.

information, and anyone (authorized) should be allowed to read it. There could be no central control.[13]

To demonstrate the concept of the World Wide Web, Berners-Lee and colleague Robert Cailliau attended a hypertext convention at a San Antonio, Texas, hotel in November 1991. They convinced the hotel to run a telephone line to their demonstration area and enlisted the aid of the Internet-savvy staff at the nearby University of Texas at San Antonio to allow them to use their dial-in service to access CERN's server. While this arrangement only allowed them to demonstrate how the Web worked on CERN's system, the demonstration was a milestone. Berners-Lee notes that at that same conference two years later, "every [demonstration] would have something to do with the Web."[14]

The World Wide Web Goes Mainstream

The Internet began to enter the public's awareness in the early 1990s. Articles in mainstream media, like the *New York Times,* were drawing attention to the concept of being able to access information in unprecedented ways.

Netscape Navigator was a breakthrough browser since instead of slowly loading all content at the same time it loaded text as soon as the connection was established, while graphics loaded as the connection allowed.

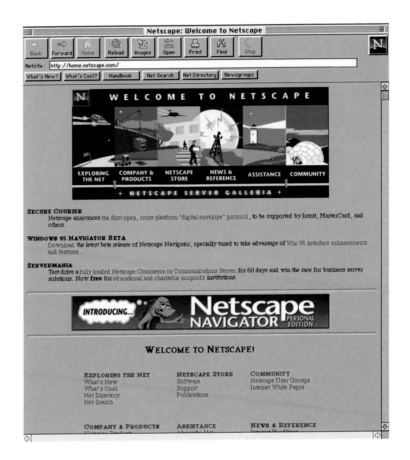

At the same time, a number of enthusiasts developed more user-friendly browsers to more effectively navigate the Internet.

The most efficient of these was created by University of Illinois students Marc Andreessen and Eric Bina as part of an undergraduate project. They called their new browser "Mosaic." What made Mosaic more effective than earlier browsers, and consequently more popular among both computer-savvy and nontechnical users alike, was that it was easy to install and easy to learn. Because many early Web pages were mostly text (even small photographs could take minutes to download through early Internet connections), early browsers displayed images in separate windows. Mosaic was the first browser to display graphics in line with accompanying text. In addition, Mosaic ran not only on the Unix-based servers found in scientific communities, but, in later versions, it also ran on Macintosh and Microsoft Windows platforms that were becoming popular for home and office use.

Mosaic's graphic user interface (GUI) set the standard for point-and-click navigation of the Internet. After college, Andreessen formed Netscape Communications, a company that made Mosaic commercially available, and it became wildly popular. In the October 1994 issue of *Wired* magazine, Gary Wolfe describes how using Mosaic enabled users to "travel through the online world along paths of whim and intuition." He also writes, "Mosaic is . . . the most pleasurable way [to find information], and in the 18 months since it was released, Mosaic has incited a rush of excitement and commercial energy unprecedented in the history of the Net."[15]

The spread of Mosaic was accompanied by a surge in servers on the Web. When Mosaic debuted in January 1993, there were fifty public servers on the Web. By October 1993 that number had risen to more than five hundred, and by the following June, it was over fifteen hundred. Clearly, the World Wide Web was catching on.

Two months after Wolfe's article appeared in *Wired*, Netscape Communications released the Netscape Navigator browser. One of Navigator's innovations was that it loaded a Web page's text as soon as the connection was established, with graphics loading as the network connection allowed. In earlier browsers, a user had to wait until the page's entire contents were loaded before anything was visible, often seeing a blank screen for minutes at a time. Navigator's advancements made browsing faster and more enjoyable.

Enhanced Security

By 1995 the first generation of the World Wide Web experience—what today is called Web 1.0—existed. Netscape Navigator worked on Unix, Windows, and Macintosh platforms. Microsoft's Internet Explorer browser arrived that same year. More and more servers and Web pages were coming online, offering content as varied as an enthusiast's list of his favorite books to works of art from the Vatican. And Berners-Lee's concept of the Web—"not a physical 'thing' that existed in a certain 'place' [but a] 'space' in which information could exist"[16]—was becoming a reality.

Also in 1995 Netscape debuted secure sockets layer (SSL), a protocol that provided enhanced security in computer communications. SSL added encryption to the data stream and paved the way for the commercialization of the Web.

Adding SSL to a commercial Web site offered security to both the owner of the site and the visitor who wished to make a financial transaction online. SSL ensured that the user's information, such as credit card numbers and expiration dates, were encrypted during transmission. Commercial sites took advantage of this new technology and commercial Web sites sprang up by the thousands. Two of them became hallmarks of the Web 1.0 experience.

The Web Goes Commercial

A commercial Web site originally called AuctionNet debuted in 1995. It was the brainchild of Pierre Omidyar, who ran Echo Bay Technology Group in San Jose, California. The first item sold on his site was a broken laser pointer for $14.83. Omidyar wanted to call his first Web site echobay.com, but found that the name had been bought by a mining company. So he chose a shortened version, eBay.com, instead. In 1996 eBay hosted 250,000 auctions; in 1997, the number of auctions skyrocketed to 2 million.

Another debut came from entrepreneur Jeff Bezos, who wanted to start an online bookstore. With the belief that an online bookstore could offer more titles than any actual bookstore in a mall, Bezos began his Web site in July 1995. He called it Amazon.com, after the South American river with the world's largest water flow. The site's first sale

Jeff Bezos began the online bookstore Amazon in 1995 and by 1997 sales were more than $147 million.

came later that month, and after six months, sales reached $500,000. According to the *New York Times,* Amazon.com "was soon posting the kind of gaudy growth rates that impress Wall Street: sales hit $15.7 million in 1996 and $147.8 million in 1997."[17]

By the end of 1997, there were more than 19.5 million hosts on the Internet worldwide. The total was almost twice as many as had been online in 1996 and was more than three times the number that had existed at the end of 1995. With all those users online, entrepreneurs offered a variety of ways for people to find what they wanted on the Web.

Rise of the Search Engines

During the early days of Web 1.0, there were two ways to navigate to a Web page. Typing in the URL was one way and finding a page through a link from another page was the other. This second method gave rise to the search engine, in which a service attempted to index all the Web pages in existence and match them to a user's request. Users discovered that their searches needed to be specific and succinct—the fewer words the better. A search for "New York restaurants" could generate a list of Web pages that had any of the three words in their titles or contents.

During the late 1990s, a number of search engines debuted as sites that were independent from the search function inside browsers. Sites like AltaVista, Yahoo!, and MetaCrawler not only boasted more complete search results, but also offered categories to narrow down a search, so that a user could select a category, such as "Food" or "Entertainment," when searching for "New York restaurants."

In 1998 they were joined by another search engine. The site's GUI had a simple, colorful, one-word logo on a plain white background; some links to site information; and a search box. This search engine was the brainchild of Larry Page and Sergey Brin, PhD students at Stanford University and was originally called "Google!" (a takeoff on the number googol, or 1×10^{100}), as a means of expressing how many results were available through its search engine. Users were impressed and pleased by Google's results and were particularly intrigued by its "I'm feeling lucky" button underneath the search box, which took users to a random site loosely connected to their search parameters. Web surfers began to use its services in unprecedented numbers such that other search engines faded into obscurity, or moved into other services (such as news services or e-mail hosting). In addition, the site's name became a verb; "to google" became synonymous with "to look up."

No matter how sophisticated these search engines were—by the end of 1998, Google was able to search an index of 60 million Web pages—their content was still defined by their developers. Users remained unable to interact with or affect the content. However, the era of user-defined content was on the horizon.

Shawn Fanning, Napster, and User-Driven Content

In 1999 Shawn Fanning was a nineteen-year-old college dropout in Massachusetts with a dream. He was frustrated with his inability to find quality music on the Internet. He

With the founding of Napster, Shawn Fanning brought a new kind of user to the Web, a person interested in the concept of sharing content.

was tired of putting music on his computer in what had become the traditional way—ripping music from CDs as MP3 files. He wanted a way for people to search for and share the music they liked.

After endless hours spent writing code, Fanning released a program called Napster, which revolutionized how music was shared. In an October 2000 profile of Fanning in *Time*, writer Karl Taro Greenfeld proclaimed, "In terms of users, the Napster site is the fastest growing in history, recently passing the 25 million mark in less than a year of operation. . . . For its users, Napster has become another appliance, like a toaster or washing machine. Call it the music appliance: log on, download, play songs. The simplicity of the program is part of its genius."[18]

Despite Napster's popularity with the public, many recording artists and the recording industry in general felt that such methods of sharing music violated their copyrights. They argued that because users were not paying for the music they were downloading, they were denying artists their royalties and companies their profits. Napster's lawyers contended that the music was only being shared, which was allowed under the Audio Home Recording Act of 1992, and that Napster was not selling the music or even storing it on their servers.

The courts eventually found in favor of the artists and the recording industry, and Napster, as a free service, was forced to shut down in 2001. However, Napster's legacy may be that it exposed a larger group of Web users to the concept of sharing content. Users began to speculate that other people on the Internet might be interested in the same things they were.

Beyond Mere Content

While one avenue for user-driven content was closed when Napster was shuttered in 2001, another opened with the arrival of Wikipedia. A conversation between Internet entrepreneur Jimmy Wales and online encyclopedia pioneer Larry Sanger about building an encyclopedia based on community submission led to the concept of a free and community-based online collaboration. They called it "Wikipedia," using the Hawaiian word *wiki* (which means "fast") as its root. Wiki was first used in a computing sense by Ward Cunningham to describe "the simplest online database that could possibly work."[19]

Wales and Sanger expanded the wiki concept into an online encyclopedia, and in the first two months of its existence, Wikipedia received almost 3,000 articles. That number reached 20,000 after its first year; by the start of its second, the project had ballooned to more than 100,000 articles in nearly 30 languages. By March 2010 there were over 3.2 million articles in English alone, and wikis in more than 250 other languages.

Beyond Wikipedia's hallmark of user-driven submissions was its encouragement of user editing. Readers were encouraged to edit the pages written by others to increase accuracy, update links, and clarify content and concepts. Users found the process easy and rewarding. The site's text editor enabled users to edit the content immediately or to upload properly formatted text imported from a user's offline word processing program.

Wikipedia's success as a community effort—in which information came from many people into a single forum—

contrasted with existing information outlets, such as online encyclopedias and news media sites. The breadth and depth of topics on Wikipedia, as well as the speed at which information about current events was posted, led observers to muse that the future of the Web would be driven by its many users and not by a few content developers.

The Coming of Web 2.0

The advances in interactivity on the World Wide Web had not escaped the notice of those who were watching the Web for glimpses of the Internet's future. Web designer Darcy DiNucci coined the phrase *Web 2.0* in an article in *Print* magazine in July 1999. DiNucci looked at current technology and considered future applications, writing, "The Web we know now, which loads into a window on our computer screens in essentially static screenfuls, is an embryo of the Web to come. The first glimmerings of Web 2.0 are now beginning to appear, and we are just starting to see how that embryo might develop." She went on to imagine that Web 2.0 would serve as "a transport mechanism, the ether through which interactivity happens. It will still appear on your computer screen, transformed by video and other dynamic media made possible by the speedy connection technologies now coming down the pike."[20]

By the early 2000s, DiNucci's speculations were becoming reality, as more and more aspects of the Internet experience were becoming interactive. In 2004 technology designers, Internet enthusiasts, and social observers met in the first-ever "Web 2.0 Conference" in San Francisco, California. Organizers John Batelle and Tim O'Reilly shared their vision for the future of Web 2.0, believing that the key was to understand the concept of "the Web as platform." In other words, they advocated the development of software that was able to avoid conflicts that exist across computer platforms (such as between Microsoft and Apple operating systems) and that took advantage of Internet connectivity. They advocated participatory architecture, in which Web sites encouraged user submissions and feedback, and counseled that designers must be able to control their own data.

As the decade progressed, the differences between Web 1.0 sites and Web 2.0 sites became more pronounced. Designers and programmers who had spent their formative years with the Internet always at their fingertips were rethinking the information and entertainment environments, and reexamining how individuals interact and stay in touch. Their efforts changed the Internet experience for millions around the world.

CHAPTER 2

The New News

In the first years of the twenty-first century, the Internet was reaching millions of people around the globe. But users were limited in how they could share their own experiences with others, especially when it came to news and events they found important. Web 1.0 sites offered few options in this area; however, developers of Web 2.0 applications began to investigate ways in which Internet users could follow, share, and react to the world around them as never before.

Traditional Media Goes Online

As the popularity of the Internet expanded in the 1990s, countless businesses created a presence on the Web. Many of these belonged to what became known as the traditional media, which includes radio and television stations, as well as newspapers and magazines. For example, the Web site for the *Boston Globe* newspaper, boston.com, arrived in October 1995; the *New York Times'* Web site, NYTimes.com, followed in January 1996. Web sites for *Time* and *Newsweek* magazines launched in December 1998.

These sites included much of the content that had made the paper publications successful: investigative reporting, editorials, sports, and community-based special interest stories, as well as breaking national and international news. News

magazine Web sites began to offer updates on the stories in their weekly paper publications, as well as interviews and behind-the-scenes looks connected with the magazines' major articles. Newspaper Web sites offered immediacy unmatched by traditional paper publishing; readers no longer had to wait for the next day's edition to keep current with the news.

As the years passed, the Web sites of some newspapers competed with or supplanted their own print edition. More and more readers relied on the Internet for their news, and circulation numbers for newspapers throughout the United States declined sharply in the first decade of the twenty-first century. To combat the resulting drops in revenue, some companies curtailed their community-based operations; the *Los Angeles Times* ceased publication of several Los Angeles County–based editions and special-interest sections from 2001 to 2006. Some companies opted for a Web-dominant existence; the Ann Arbor, Michigan, *News* reduced its

Sharing Opinions

The increasingly interactive nature of Web 2.0 is particularly visible when readers express opinions about stories on news sites. Stories involving politics or political figures, in particular, provoke readers to submit their comments and add their voice to the debate at hand.

But sometimes, stories about small communities or individuals generate tremendous interest. For example, on March 11, 2010, a story about a small town in Mississippi became the talk of Web 2.0. The Itawamba County school board canceled the high school prom because a gay student, Constance McMillen, wished to wear a tuxedo instead of a dress and take her girlfriend as her date to the dance.

What would have remained a local issue in the years before the Internet quickly became the topic of tweets and social network posts across Web 2.0. Users waded in with their opinions; for example, on Newsvine, an interactive site where readers can post their thoughts and reactions, there were more than 1400 comments in over 450 different conversations in less than 48 hours. Individuals in support of the school board created a Facebook page to express their views. Readers of Tonic.com, a site dedicated to "promoting the good that happens around the world each day," raised thirty thousand dollars toward McMillen's college expenses.

Tonic.com, "About Tonic," www.tonic.com/about.

publication to twice a week, moving the bulk of its information to the Web site. And some ceased paper printing altogether; the *Seattle Post-Intelligencer* stopped publishing in March 2009 after nearly 150 years, in favor of an online version.

Limited Reach

While interest in print versions of newspapers declined, interest in their Web versions increased. But the online stories still had a circulation similar to that of the print version; their reach was limited to those who knew about the site.

THE INTERNET AT THE POLLS

Since its introduction to the public in the 1990s, the Internet has played a large role in many elements of American society. Recently, Web 2.0 applications have begun to show new possibility within the political arena. In the 2008 U.S. presidential election, internet news sources and grassroots social networking campaigns had an unexpected impact, and for the first time the Internet surpassed newspapers in a poll tracking the primary sources of campaign news.

First source mentioned	1992	1996	2000	2004	2007
Television	68	73	68	68	60
Newspaper	20	15	15	15	12
Internet	**0**	**1**	**4**	**6**	**15**
Radio	8	8	8	7	8
Magazines	2	1	2	1	2
Other	1	1	2	1	1
Don't Know	1	1	1	2	2

Data: From Pew Research Center, January 11, 2008, "Internet's Broader Role."
http://people-press.org/report/384/internets-broader-role-in-campaign-2008

As more and more news outlets developed a presence on the Web, news sites in general experienced increased readership. Radio stations, particularly those with all-news formats, began developing Web sites to share up-to-the-minute information unavailable through radio, such as images from traffic cameras. Television stations created sites for their local news broadcasts, with links for more information about nightly stories.

Web surfers helped direct traffic to these sites through a variety of Web 1.0 techniques. They distributed news and views they found interesting by e-mailing links to the stories to their friends or by discussing them on their personal Web sites. These sites, called blogs (which is a contraction of "Web" and "logs"), enabled people from all walks of life and with all manner of opinions to share their views and stories. However, both e-mail and blogs had limited reach. If you were not on an e-mail list or did not know about a particular blog, you might miss out on a wealth of information.

The companies that operate these news outlets continue to employ journalists who dig deep into stories around the world. But it took the tinkering of a television production assistant and self-described computer geek to bring the news into the world of Web 2.0.

Digging It

In 2002 Kevin Rose, a twenty-seven-year-old Las Vegas, Nevada, native, took a job as a production assistant for a cable channel called TechTV in San Francisco. When he found a previously unknown security flaw in the Windows operating system, the producer of the *Screen Savers* program put him on the air to discuss his findings. Soon Rose's computer tips became a regular feature of the program.

At the same time, Rose was working on an idea to improve sharing news and entertainment stories beyond posting links on a Web site or a blog. He was frustrated by having to visit site after site in search of stories that piqued his interest. He wanted a way for other enthusiasts to enjoy what he liked and a way to enjoy what they liked. The result of his efforts was a site called Digg that debuted in November 2004.

What made Digg different from other sites was its social aspect. Readers could post links to stories they liked, and other readers could vote on them. They could approve of the story (or "digg" it) or disapprove of it (or "bury" it). The more "diggs" a story received, the higher it appeared in the rankings on Digg's home page.

In 2009 Digg had more than 38 million unique visitors and more than 105 million visits. But Rose is quick to point out that Digg does not stand alone from traditional news Web sites, such as NYTimes.com. In an interview with the business technology Web site ZDNet, Rose was asked if Digg

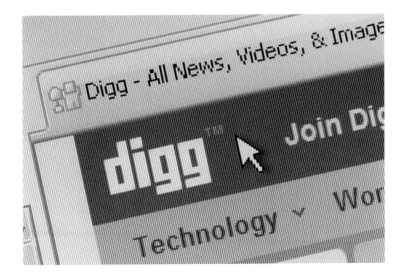

A screen shot for the Web site Digg.com which debuted in November 2004. This site was different from other news sharing sites because it allowed users to post links to news stories and other readers to vote on these stories.

would replace the *New York Times*. He replied, "We have a symbiotic relationship with traditional media sites. We can't survive unless bloggers blog and the *New York Times* writes stories. We create a level playing field [and] good content gets found and recognized."[21]

Social Media

Today Digg is not alone at discovering and sharing worthwhile content. There are many other sites, such as Mixx, reddit, and Delicious, where readers can submit, comment on, and vote on the popularity of stories from around the world. News and entertainment sites have also created areas on their sites where readers can leave comments. Additionally, some sites enable readers to share stories more easily by clicking a Digg or reddit button next to the text.

This trend toward soliciting feedback is part of the new nature of news called social media. Joseph Thornley, a public relations and marketing consultant in Toronto, Ontario, Canada, defines social media as "online communications in which individuals shift fluidly and flexibly between the role of audience and author. To do this, they use social software that enables anyone without knowledge of coding, to post, comment on, [or share] content and to form communities around shared interests."[22]

What makes news and views on Web 2.0 social media sites different from Web 1.0 news sites is the fluidity and flexibility—the changing and shifting that is similar to the ebb and flow of a good conversation with friends. Views are exchanged, opinions are challenged, and topics shift to something new. Additionally, Web users have the ability to see and read the opinions of others; they can choose to join the conversation if they wish. They can add comments or link to a story that supports or rebuts another user's post.

Many of these conversations took the form of short bursts of commentary back and forth. In many ways, these comments are similar to text messages sent via cell phone that take a short time to write and less time to read. And it was these staccato bursts of information that was the inspiration for one of the breakthrough services of Web 2.0.

"Just Setting Up My Twttr"

In 2006 a group of employees at a communications company in San Francisco called Odeo Inc. were trying to work through a creative slump. One member of the group, Jack Dorsey, had a background in instant messaging and Web-based dispatching services for taxis and couriers. He recognized that text messaging via "Short Message Service" (or "SMS") technology was increasingly popular among cell phone users in the United States. He wondered if it would be possible to send text messages to a small group of individuals at once, instead of just one person at a time.

Dorsey and the others first thought of calling the new type of texting "Twitch," after the way a cell phone behaves in vibrate mode. According to Dorsey, they rejected it,

> because it doesn't bring up the right imagery. So we looked in the dictionary for words around it, and we came across the word "twitter," and it was just perfect. The definition was "a short burst of inconsequential information," and "chirps from birds." And that's exactly what the product was.
>
> The whole bird thing: bird chirps sound meaningless to us, but meaning is applied by other birds. The

The use of Twitter has skyrocketed since it was introduced in 2006. The site was even used by Barack Obama during his successful campaign to become president of the United States.

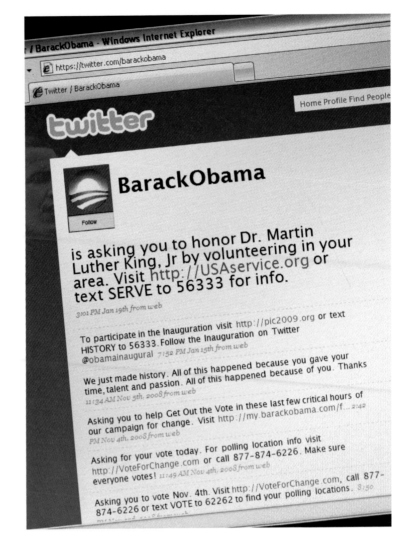

same is true of Twitter: a lot of messages can be seen as completely useless and meaningless, but it's entirely dependent on the recipient. So we just fell in love with the word.[23]

Twitter debuted publicly in November 2006. Its first message, written by Dorsey, was "just setting up my twttr."[24]

A Twitter posting, called a tweet, is limited to 140 characters. Dorsey envisioned it as a service that was most effective via cell phones. Today Twitter users share information

TWITTER – BY THE NUMBERS

In April 2010 Twitter cofounder Biz Stone revealed that the social networking site had recorded more than 105 million users, just four years after its launch in March 2006. The company also shared that they were registering around 300,000 new users per day. Despite the staggering numbers, Twitter is still primarily a U.S. phenomenon.

COUNTRY	% OF TWITTER USERS
USA	62.14
UK	7.87
Canada	5.69
Australia	2.80
Brazil	2.00
Germany	1.51
India	.87
South Africa	.85
Japan	.71
Sweden	.54
China	.49

Data: Information from "Twitter User Statistics Revealed," Huffington Post, (April 14, 2010). http://www.huffingtonpost.com/2010/04/14/twitter-user-statistics-r_n_537992.html.

from any Web-connected device, including laptops and cell phones. These bursts of condensed information being passed back and forth across the Twitter network, called the Twitter stream or the Twitterverse, led to a change in how Web 2.0 users shared their news. Twitter users began to share all sorts of information, current events to traffic conditions to their daily menu choices. Users sent out more than 1.2 billion tweets in January 2010, which was an all-time high for the service. This practice of condensed bursts of news, views, and links is known as microblogging.

Microblogging

A microblog, such as Twitter, is distinguished from a traditional blog by how much information is shared by an individual at any one time. Instead of having the unrestricted space of a blog in which to express one's views and opinions, a microblogger on Twitter is obliged to be quite succinct due to the 140-character limit. Some microbloggers have adopted many of the shorthand abbreviations that are popular in text messaging. Some, such as "LOL" or "IDK," are familiar to many Web 2.0 users; others are less so. For example, after Leigh Mills of WMTV in Madison, Wisconsin, reported on an upcoming 150-mile (241-km) charity bicycle ride, she was puzzled by a response she received on her Facebook page from a teenage viewer that read "idk! lol but ily 2 death." Mills shared it with her blog's readers, concluding that it meant " 'I don't know. Laugh out loud but I love you to death.' Very sweet response from a girl, who was letting me know that she's not sure she can ride in the [charity event] but likes watching our newscasts."[25]

Since Twitter's arrival on the Web 2.0 scene, other microblogs have sprung up. Sites such as Tumblr, Plurk, and Jaiku have attracted users around the globe. Companies as well as organizations create accounts on such sites and advertise that Web users can "follow us on Twitter." In many U.S. cities, radio stations create microblogging accounts for their hosts or DJs in order to drive traffic to their Web sites or to provide more in-depth coverage of stories. For example, in Washington, D.C., radio listeners can follow microblogs on Facebook and Twitter for music station WBIG, sports talk station WTEM, and the all-news station WTOP.

For many, microblogging is at the heart of their Web 2.0 experience. They enjoy posting their ideas, photos, and comments or sharing links to interesting Web pages they have found. Others like to investigate links posted by other bloggers. And trends among active microbloggers in the United States suggest that microblogging is affecting traditional blogging statistics. According to a report published in February 2010 by the Pew Research Center, young adults are maintaining traditional blogs in fewer numbers. In 2006, 28 percent of American teen Internet users ages twelve to seventeen said they actively blogged, but a similar survey in 2009 found that number down to 14 percent. The numbers suggest that microblogging is more popular with younger Internet users. Amanda Lenhart, senior researcher at the Pew Research Center and an author of the study, believes that Twitter and similar forms of microblogging have "kind of sucked the life out of long-form blogging."[26] At the same time, Americans thirty and older are using the long form more often; the study says that 11 percent maintain a blog or a Web site.

No matter the age of the blogger, the result of all of these individuals reading and posting on the Internet is that the number of events, stories, and circumstances that get widespread attention continues to rise. And in many cases, the attention comes from individuals who are on the scene when the event unfolds.

Before the News Breaks

One of the hallmarks of being connected to the Internet is the sense of immediacy. Users feel that they are in better contact with their world than those who are not online. And one of the hallmarks of using Web 2.0 applications is being able to see the fluidity of changing events. An innovation in the early 2000s called Really Simple Syndication (RSS) enabled Web users to receive up-to-the-minute feeds from a wide variety of news sources and bloggers. For example, one blogger in San Francisco, California, configured his RSS feeds to notify him when his favorite restaurants had a reservation available on a Friday at 8 P.M.

A ferry on its way to rescue the passengers of U.S. Airways Flight 1549 after the plane had to make an emergency landing in the Hudson River in January 2009. It was a passenger on the ferry that first broke the news of the emergency landing by Tweeting about it on his cell phone.

Additional Web 2.0 innovations allow users to interact with other users to share their views as events unfold. In an interview with Andrew Lennon, the editor in chief of the technology blog The Daily Anchor, Twitter cofounder Jack Dorsey described a series of tweets he received about an earth tremor. Lennon writes,

The first message he [Dorsey] received was something along the lines of, "was that an earthquake?" followed seconds later by someone confirming the quake and guessing at the magnitude, followed by someone across town sharing their experience, followed by someone saying they just checked the USGS [U.S. Geological Survey] website and could confirm the magnitude was . . . whatever it was. In minutes rumor had turned to news, and it didn't happen with any phone calls or TV

News Anchor or "confirmed report" from the USGS, it happened on cell phones with SMS text and a nifty little program that required you to condense your sentiments into 140 characters. The authenticity of real-time individual experience had collided with cold hard facts and the bare essence of information.[27]

As the number of Web-enabled cell phones has grown worldwide, a variety of events have been documented and shared by eyewitnesses through texts, tweets, or other microblogging bursts of information. During the terrorist attacks in Mumbai, India, in November 2008, an estimated eighty tweets were sent by eyewitnesses and bloggers every five seconds. In an article for CNN, journalist Stephanie Busari writes, "Many Twitter users also sent pleas for blood donors to make their way to specific hospitals in Mumbai where doctors were faced with low stocks and rising casualties. Others sent information about helplines and contact numbers for those who had friends and relatives caught up in the attacks."[28] The first news of an airliner's emergency landing in New York's Hudson River in January 2009 came from a tweet from Janis Krums, a passenger on a ferry in the river. When the ferry changed course to aid in the rescue, he tweeted, "There's a plane in the Hudson. I'm on the ferry going to pick up the people. Crazy."[29]

In addition, these messages often have photos or a short video attached, taken by the users' cell phone. For example, Krums took a photo of the airplane as the ferry approached it and posted the image to Twitter's photo-sharing page, called Twitpic. The photo became an iconic image of the event. Videos of the emergency landing, copied from security cameras on the shoreline, also found their way onto Web sites. This type of eyewitness reporting is called citizen journalism. It has helped redefine how news events are covered around the world, as the first bits of news are sent, seen, and resent, or "retweeted," from user to user across the globe.

Unfortunately sometimes tweets and retweets contain misleading or erroneous information. For example, during the Mumbai attacks, a series of tweets were supposedly

Tweeting the Haitian Earthquake

On January 12, 2010, a devastating earthquake hit the nation of Haiti. With the global reach of Web 2.0, news of the quake spread quickly. That morning, Haitian disc jockey Carel Pedre's morning radio show was accompanied by a variety of tweets about his playlist and news of the day; but by 4 P.M., his tweets had taken on a different tone: "If U Need To get in Touch With Friends & Family in Haiti. Send me a Private Message with names and Phone Numbers. I'll get Back to U!"

Pedre's radio station, powered by generator, enabled him to keep broadcasting and tweeting in English, French, and Creole, and to document the recovery efforts.

He was by no means the only Twitter user on the scene. On January 18, CNN's medical correspondent, Sanjay Gupta, performed emergency brain surgery onboard the USS *Comfort*, although it was not his specialty. His tweet that started "attention: no neurosurgeons in haiti that can be found," galvanized a pastor in Atlanta, Georgia, to spread the word through the Twitterverse. Less than forty-eight hours later, five neurosurgeons volunteered to go to Haiti that week.

Carel Pedre, Twitter feed, January 12, 2010, quoted in Maria De Los Angeles, "Silicon Beach: Twitter Hits Ground Running for Haiti Earthquake Relief," *Miami New Times*, January 13, 2010. Available at http://blogs.miaminewtimes.com/riptide/2010/01/silicon_beach_twitter_hits_gro.php.

Sanjay Gupta, Twitter feed, January 18, 2010, quoted in Kathryn Blaze Carlson, "CNN reporter Sanjay Gupta becomes part of the story in Haiti," *The National Post*, January 18, 2010. Available at http://www.nationalpost.com/news/world/story.html?id=2461040.

sent by the Indian government asking users to stop tweeting in the name of security; these were eventually found to be hoaxes. Busari writes, "someone tweets a news headline, their friends see it and retweet, prompting an endless circle of recycled information."[30]

Mostly "Pointless Babble"

The challenge for individuals trying to follow the news is being able to decipher what is the important information within the "endless circle of recycled information." While the presence of citizen journalists on the scene of a breaking news story can be invaluable to understanding a situation as it unfolds, the vast majority of tweets are about less-than-momentous occasions. The comic strip *Doonesbury* satirized the constant tweeting that some users seem to undertake, showing a news reporter tweeting about everything he did, as he did it, including his boss coming to fire him.

According to a study by Pear Analytics of San Antonio, Texas, this type of microblogging is the predominant type of posting on Twitter. The firm studied two thousand tweets in English from varying times of day over a two-week period in August 2009. The tweets were sorted into categories that included "News," "Spam," "Conversational," and "Pointless Babble." The survey's authors report that the percentage of Conversational messages (chats that were more like texts between friends) surprised them; they were 38 percent of the total. But the clear winner was the Pointless Babble tweet; the authors call them "the 'I am eating a sandwich now' tweets."[31] The percentage of messages deemed Pointless Babble comprised nearly 41 percent of the total.

As mundane as some of these messages may seem, there are countless users of Twitter and other microblogging sites that create posts that others find interesting. These readers then choose to "follow" the bloggers, and avidly read everything they post.

BITS & BYTES

41%

Percentage of Twitter messages characterized by a Pear Analytics study as "Pointless Babble"

Airing Grievances on the Web

Occasionally a microblogger feels the need to share information that, in the days before Web 2.0, would hardly be treated as news and that some people might include in the "Pointless Babble" category. One example of this occurred on February 13, 2010. Filmmaker Kevin Smith boarded an early evening Southwest Airlines flight from Oakland, California, to Burbank, California. Smith was asked to leave the airplane by Southwest staff who told him that he was too overweight to fit safely in a seat. Smith protested, but eventually left the plane, declining the airline's offer of a one hundred dollar voucher as compensation.

Smith used his Twitter account, which has over 1.5 million followers, to air his side of the incident, addressing his tweets directly to the airline's Twitter account. He wrote over fifty tweets in two hours following the incident. His posts included several comments directed at Southwest's policies, at the pilot of the flight on which he was originally seated, and to his Twitter followers in general. When he boarded another flight to Burbank just forty-five minutes later, he tweeted that he was expecting to be removed from that flight as well.

Southwest Airlines replied directly to Smith via Twitter and by telephone. The tweets contained an apology and reflected a desire to explain their decision. They also listed

"Retweeting"

Messages that are posted on the microblogging service Twitter are called tweets. Twitter users decide which tweets they wish to follow; this process enables them to see every feed from the individual or group they are following. If a user reads a tweet that he or she then forwards on to his or her own followers, that process is called retweeting.

Retweeting is similar to forwarding an e-mail, with two main differences. The first is that the retweet joins the entire Twitter stream, and the person doing the retweeting credits the original tweet with the preface "RT" (for retweet) followed by "@" and the person's Twitter name. The remainder of the tweet is simply the original post. Business strategist and Twitter user John D. Varlaro says, "The @ ensures that I see you retweeted me as a response, while your followers see that I wrote it and can now follow me."

The most popular retweets are usually favorite articles and the most important stories of the entire Twitter community. Users find retweeting helpful when looking for important articles, reading useful blog posts, or for examining or tracking emerging trends.

John D. Varlaro, "Tweetiquette for Beginners," The Human Strategist (Web site), April 20, 2009, www.thehumanisticstrategist.com/articles/2009/4/20/tweetiquette-for-beginners.html.

a link to a press release about the incident. The statement noted that Smith had followed Southwest policy by purchasing two seats, as he had done on previous flights, but then he changed his plans, wanting to depart from Oakland on an earlier flight. This put him in stand-by status, in which all regularly ticketed passengers are seated first. According to Southwest, "when the time came to board Mr. Smith, we had only a single seat available for him to occupy. Our pilots are responsible for the Safety and comfort of all Customers on the aircraft and therefore, made the determination that Mr. Smith needed more than one seat to complete his flight."[32]

The story made headlines around the world. Television stations in California and elsewhere aired analyses of the event; one of Smith's Twitter followers said the story had been front-page news in Hungary. In less than eighteen hours, the story was being covered by international media and had prompted a press release from a major airline.

A Web 2.0 Soapbox

Kevin Smith not only used Twitter to protest his treatment by Southwest Airlines, but also to take exception to an established policy with which he had complied in the past. In the days before Web 2.0 applications, the story would likely have received less attention and certainly would not have spread around the world as quickly as it did. But Smith's decision to publicize the incident, as well as to share his personal feelings about it, turned his Twitter account into a protest platform. This is called "getting on one's soapbox," a reference to how early protesters stood on wooden crates in order to be better seen and heard by an audience.

The difference with being on a soapbox today is that one's views can spread instantaneously, and that readers often get just one side of a story. If Southwest had not had a Twitter account, Smith's tweets might have gone unnoticed by the airline. It would have been unable to directly respond in the same forum that Smith was using. And Smith's followers would have been unable to read the airline's apologies and explanations.

Smith is not the first personality to use microblogging as a soapbox. National Football League receiver Chad Ochocinco used his Twitter account in August 2009 to protest the league's new policy against tweeting before, during, and after games. He even suggested a contest in which the winner would join him at a game to post tweets in his name. Skateboarder and video game developer Tony Hawk used Twitter to try to goad German airline Lufthansa into finding his lost luggage, which included one of his custom-built skateboards.

However, some Twitter users use a Web 2.0 soapbox for less self-promoting reasons. Understanding that Twitter is reaching more and more Internet users, a variety of celebrities from the world of stage, screen, and athletics choose to put Web 2.0 to good use, by increasing awareness of worthwhile causes.

Although he originally joined Twitter for self promotion, Ashton Kutcher now realizes that he can use the microblogging site to promote good causes as well.

Tweeting for a Cause

Occasionally the Web includes celebrity-related news that relates only a portion of the story. On Tuesday, April 13, 2009, actor Ashton Kutcher tweeted that he wanted to reach 1 million followers faster than news outlet CNN's breaking news feed. At the time, no one on Twitter had that many followers. Kutcher narrowly won the race, reaching the magic number early the following Friday morning.

The competition was news across the Twitterverse and in traditional media circles as well. Some critics decried its self-promotional aspect, but others pointed out that Kutcher had pledged to donate ten thousand mosquito bed nets to charity on World Malaria Day on April 25 if he won or one thousand if he lost. (Although CNN lost the race, they also donated ten thousand bed nets.)

Kutcher admitted that he first joined Twitter as a way of promoting himself, but then discovered that his tweets could do much more. In an interview on the CNN television show *Larry King Live,* he said,

At the end of the day, we all have ego, we all have some level of ego. But if we can use our ego to actually create good charitable things in the world in some way, and use our ego—originally, I defined Twitter as an ego stream when I first saw it. But then what I realized is if we can transform that into something that's positive that can actually effectively change the world, that can be a really valuable tool.[33]

Since then, other personalities have joined Twitter and other microblogging sites to promote appearances, concerts, book signings, and their favorite causes. Following the January 2010 earthquakes in Haiti, Rachelle Lefevre, an actress best known for her roles in the *Twilight* movie series, encouraged her fans to support the Red Cross through blood donations. Additionally, Lefevre donates $100 to Susan G. Komen for the Cure, a breast cancer research charity, for every ten thousand followers she gains on Twitter; she had donated nearly $3,000 by May 2010. Professional cyclist and cancer survivor Lance Armstrong founded the cancer awareness and prevention foundation LIVESTRONG and uses Twitter to promote fitness for all ages and to comment on sports. Comedian and game show host Drew Carey has pledged $1 million to LIVESTRONG based on how many Twitter followers he gains. By June 2010, he had already donated $450,000.

Is It News?

These celebrities and other microblog users have challenged the definition of what is news. An item about a new tweak to the Linux computer operating system will garner comments from Linux enthusiasts but few others. A story about a natural disaster will likely receive broader dissemination, with millions of readers passing it on to their contacts and posting it for others to see. But each represents the nature of the new news on Web 2.0.

The increasingly interactive nature of the Internet allows users to customize it to suit their tastes, instead of having to wade through items that do not interest them. Mike Laurie, a creative arts designer and writer for the London, England–based agency Made By Many, is convinced that the new news represents a fundamental shift in how we perceive events. He writes, "We're no longer lazy consumers of passive messages. Instead we're active participants. We now get news through the network *we've* created, and the news we pass to one another says something about us. It tells others what we're interested in and what's important to us."[34]

The new news also means that, as they surf the Web, users may find that they share interests with other people using the same service. Striking up an Internet-based conversation can lead to shared information, opinions, and new perspectives. It can also lead to interpersonal connections undreamed of until the advent of Web 2.0.

CHAPTER 3

Social Networks

T he evolution of the World Wide Web has led to unprecedented opportunities for communications and information exchange. Millions of people around the world create billions of text messages, tweets, and other blog posts. Many write for the love of the written word; they enjoy sharing their observations and crafting phrases that may appeal only to them and a few friends. Others share whatever comes into their heads at any given time. Few of these individuals will become famous, unless something they see or do puts them at the right place at the right time. Janis Krums, the ferry passenger who sent out the first tweet about the 2009 Hudson River airplane landing, became famous for a short time. He gained thousands of followers to his Twitter feeds as a result of his tweets and photo of the event.

However, one does not need to be famous to have a presence on Web 2.0. In fact, one of the benefits of Web 2.0 applications is that almost anyone can take advantage of user-driven content. Many users become part of a Web 2.0 innovation that enables people to be connected as never before. These Internet communities are called social networks. Today such networks provide Web-based forums for a myriad of special interest groups, commercial interests, and government agencies. And each is driven by the desire for information.

Meeting and Connecting

The social networks of Web 2.0 are the descendants of Web 1.0 applications called bulletin boards and listservs. Both services were comprised of a community of individuals with common interests, such as electronic games, computing innovations, or humor. These services had areas on their sites called chat rooms, where users could read and respond to what other members were writing.

By the mid-1990s, entrepreneurs were trying to take this concept of community one step further. A service called Classmates.com arrived in 1995, which offered individuals a way to find former schoolmates. SixDegrees, which debuted in 1997, was the first service to allow users to create

A screen shot of the social networking site Friendster, which was created in 2002 by Jonathan Abrams. The site was so successful that within six months after launch it had attracted 3 million registered users.

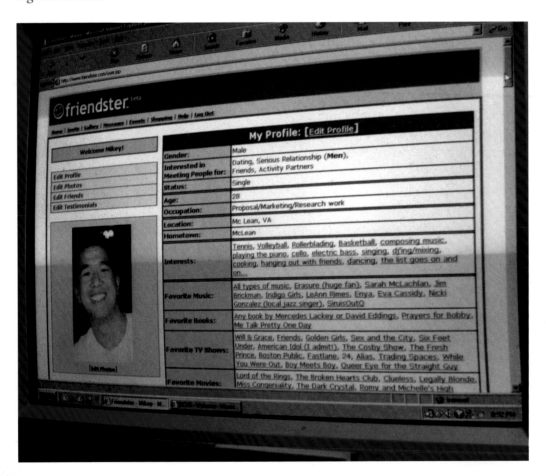

their own profile, or personal description that included such information as age, religion, and hometown, and to allow them to list their friends. Thirty-two-year-old Jonathan Abrams, a former engineer at Netscape, developed Friendster in 2002 as a way to meet his friends' friends. According to one of the company's early investors, "basically, Jonathan wanted to meet girls. He told me himself, he started Friendster as a way to surf through his friends' address books for good-looking girls."[35] Friendster was so successful that it attracted 3 million registered users within six months.

Several Friendster account holders employed by an Internet marketing company decided to create their own social network. MySpace rolled out in August 2003, and within two years it had surpassed Friendster in registered users. By 2006 Friendster had stagnated while MySpace was thriving. According to *New York Times* writer Gary Rivlin, one of the differences between Friendster and MySpace was how the networks worked. He writes, "Users at Friendster could view only the profiles of those on a relatively short chain of acquaintances. By contrast, MySpace was open, and therefore much simpler from a technological standpoint; anybody could look at anyone else's profile."[36]

MySpace also encouraged profiles from entities other than individuals, such as clubs and rock bands, which Friendster did not allow. Clubs posted upcoming events, and bands advertised new concert dates, leading to their fans interacting and expanding the network.

The success of Friendster, MySpace, and others led to additional social network sites showing up around the world, and there are now hundreds of them from which to choose. Some are more popular in particular areas; for example, Bebo is popular in Great Britain and Europe, Orkut is popular in South America, and Qzone is popular in China. However, by 2010, all of these were eclipsed by a

BITS & BYTES
4,000
Approximate number of users who joined Facebook in its first two weeks of operation in 2004

program started by a college student who had just been rejected by a young woman.

"The Facebook"

On October 28, 2003, a Harvard University sophomore named Mark Zuckerberg was blogging in his dorm room about how he had just been dumped and how he was trying to get the woman off his mind. He started looking through a Harvard publication on his table, nicknamed "the facebook," which had photographs of students in his dormitory. The publication was a way for students to get to know each other. Zuckerberg thought that some of the photos were, in his words, "pretty horrendous."[37] He thought about creating a site where he would post pictures side by side and invite readers to rate the photos.

He hacked into Harvard's database to retrieve school ID photos, and he worked on it all that night, blogging as he went. He called it "Facemash," and it was wildly popular on campus. It was a Web-based version of the Harvard game, Hot or Not, in which students rated the appeal of members of the opposite sex based on photographs. News of the site spread quickly, as students e-mailed each other about it, and that first night, more than 450 signed on, generating twenty-two-thousand page views. University administration, however, was not amused; within a few hours, it had traced the site to Zuckerberg and cut off his Internet access. He was later accused of violating Harvard's student privacy policy and downloading college property, but the charges were eventually dropped.

Facemash inspired Zuckerberg to create a way to get Harvard students to meet and interact with each other, as other Web 2.0 applications were doing. Throughout the next few months, he spent countless hours programming his dream. He launched a new site, called "The Facebook," on March 4, 2004. About four thousand people signed up in the first two weeks, and news of the site began to spread to other universities. Part of the site's appeal was that users needed a legitimate college e-mail address (one ending in ".edu") to sign up; students recognized that The Facebook's community was limited to people their own age and to those in the college communities.

"Facebook Was the Best to Come Along"

By the time Harvard's term ended on May 28, The Facebook had nearly two hundred thousand users at thirty colleges nationwide. According to Claire Hoffman, who profiled Zuckerberg in the June 26, 2008, issue of *Rolling Stone* magazine, "college students, it seemed, were eager to use Zuckerberg's invention obsessively, to share their most personal details online."[38] Jeff Jarvis, director of the interactive journalism program at the City University of New York, noted that Facebook (the "The" was dropped in 2005) "was better than its predecessors. Friendster was a game; MySpace was a tacky home page. Facebook was the best to come along."[39]

In September 2005 Facebook expanded to allow high school students to sign up through an invitation-only network, and a year later, it was opened to anyone fourteen or older who had a valid e-mail address. People were attracted by its simple and uncluttered graphic user interface and the ability to customize profiles to include as little or as much

Due to its simple and uncluttered interface and its ability to customize profiles, people began to leave MySpace and switch to Facebook. By mid-2007 Facebook became the most popular social networking site in the United States.

information as users wished. Additionally, Facebook users enjoyed two features not available on MySpace. Facebook's feeds allowed users to keep track of what they had posted or who had accepted a friend request, as well as to receive updates on their friends' activities. And students loved the ability to upload dozens of photographs at a time via their cell phones or their computers.

By the middle of 2007, technology observers began to label Facebook as the successor to MySpace as the leading social network. Writer Ben Gold thought that Facebook had already overtaken MySpace. He writes, "MySpace was a great social network for a while, but now there are too many spammers and the developers have stopped innovating. Facebook is just starting to become popular (well, popular with those who were not on it when it was limited to schools). So, you might want to check it out, while it's still cool."[40]

Regardless of whether or not Facebook would lose its "cool" factor as it became more popular, it was already proving to be a valuable tool for its subscribers. Some continued to use it for posting notices and photos of parties and school activities. Others discovered it had unexpected capabilities for keeping in touch across the globe.

A Multitude of Uses

At the heart of Facebook is the concept of social networking. Clay D. Hysell is a Facebook user and assistant dean for graduate services at the University of Virginia's Graduate School of Nursing. His duties include course planning, financial aid assistance, recruiting students, and developing requirements for the graduate degree program. He signed up for Facebook "back in the .edu days,"[41] when it was restricted to those in college or university communities. Over the years, Hysell has used Facebook for a wide variety of university-related duties. Recently he used it for corresponding with a prospective student from the nation of Jordan to answer the student's questions about obtaining a visa to enter the United States. He finds Facebook particularly valuable when working with university colleagues from overseas. He looks on his Facebook page to see if a particular colleague is online and then sends a message. For example, he says, "I'll send a message to a colleague in New Zealand to ask what a passing grade is there,"[42] to ensure that prospective students meet the university's standards. For him, Facebook has replaced instant messaging or texting. "It's far more efficient than sending a two-sentence e-mail,"[43] because he usually gets a response within minutes.

His network of friends on Facebook currently includes approximately one hundred current and prospective students and sixty to seventy professional colleagues. But Hysell also uses Facebook for recreation. He particularly enjoys some of the online games, and he estimates that 50 to 60 percent of the friends on his account were made through them. He also enjoys keeping up and getting back in contact with friends from his school days.

In many ways, Hysell's use of Facebook is exactly what Mark Zuckerberg envisioned when he started it: a means for networking and for maintaining and creating new

Friending and Unfriending

For many Facebook users, one of the most important aspects of the social network is the ability to find new people with similar interests and invite them to join their circle of friends. To do so, the user sends an invitation called a friend request. This process, called friending, originated with the social network called Friendster, which debuted in 2003.

When an individual initiates the friending process, the recipient receives a notice from Facebook, giving the recipient the option to accept or reject the friend request. The decision rests solely with the recipient. If the recipient accepts the request, the sender receives confirmation that the recipient has been added as a friend. From that point on, the two users can see each other's posts and send messages across the network.

Occasionally users decide to reduce the number of individuals in their network through a process called unfriending. In this process, however, the individual being unfriended receives no notification of the process; the individual simply no longer has access to the person who initiated the action.

friendships. In fact, Facebook is now the most popular social network in the world, with 500 million subscribers as of July 2010. The expanding nature of the Internet and the increasingly interactive capacity of Web 2.0 have enabled Hysell and millions of other Facebook users to connect and stay in touch as never before. However, Facebook's huge numbers do not mean it is the best social network for everyone. And because the hallmarks of Web 2.0 are personalization and user-driven content, there is a social network for just about every taste.

A Social Network for Everyone

Today there are hundreds of social networks on the Internet. There are networks that cater to people who speak languages other than English. For example, to enjoy LunarStorm, users need to understand the Swedish language, and to use the features of Vkontakte, users need to understand Russian. Language buffs can learn both Russian and Swedish through the social network italki, which enables novices to network with native speakers and paid instructors. Enthusiasts from a wide range of hobbies and lifestyles can find social networks where they can connect with users with similar interests. For example, MomsLikeMe.com and BabyCenter cater to mothers and LibraryThing and Shelfari attract book lovers.

Job seekers can take advantage of social networks in search of the perfect employer or a new career. Social media trainer Laurie Boettcher of Eau Claire, Wisconsin, uses LinkedIn, a social network that has more than 45 million users representing 150 occupations around the world. She notes that LinkedIn "is where professionals use social networking. It's an amazing tool; it allows users like you and I to maintain online resumes."[44] LinkedIn's networking ability enables employers to contact applicants and their supervisors for additional information. Additionally business owners

> ## BITS & BYTES
> ### 250,000
> Facebook users who became fans of the page "One Million Voices Against FARC" in its first month in 2008

Although Facebook and MySpace are the most used social networking Web sites in the United States, there are a number of similar applications that draw users from around the world.

Site Most Popular In

Bebo
United Kingdom

V Kontakte
Russia

Hyves
Netherlands

Facebook, MySpace
United States

Mixi
Japan

Hi5 varied:
Mexico, Peru, Dom. Rep., Mongolia, Thailand

Iwiw
Hungary

Orkut
Brazil, India, Estonia

QQ
China

Skyrock
Guadelope, Martinique

Friendster
Philippines

can learn about resources that are trusted by members of their network, such as investors or advertising agencies.

Citizens around the world have also discovered that social networks can help disseminate information about local events and community concerns. One Facebook user in rural North Carolina routinely uses it to inform her neighbors when local trash pickup is changing due to weather or holidays. But Facebook has also been used to get out the word about much larger issues.

Many Interests, Many Causes

Social networks have enabled concerned citizens to rally like-minded people to their cause. On January 4, 2008, a few Facebook users created a group on the site calling for a protest in Colombia's capital, Bogotá. Colombian engineer Oscar Morales Guevara and his colleagues called for a rally on February 4 to protest the continued actions of the antigovernment group FARC. Since the 1960s, FARC has led a guerilla-type campaign in Colombia, kidnapping individuals from Colombia and other nations, including the United States, and holding them hostage in the jungle, sometimes for years.

On February 4, 2008, hundreds of people in more than one hundred cities marched in opposition to the anti-government group FARC after a successful Facebook campaign called for the protest to take place.

Guevara's group called its Facebook page "One Million Voices Against FARC." According to the British Broadcasting Company, "over 250,000 Facebook users signed on, and the movement was taken up by newspapers and radio and television stations across [Colombia]."[45] On the day of the protest, citizens in more than one hundred cities across the world, from Washington, D.C. to Sydney, Australia, joined approximately 1 million Colombians to march against FARC.

Another striking example of social networking's power and potential was Barack Obama's successful campaign for U.S. president. The candidate's team established accounts on Facebook, MySpace, BlackPlanet.com, and other social network sites to spread the word about Obama's campaign. In addition, the campaign team created My.BarackObama.com, a social network on which more than 2 million supporters and volunteers coordinated online and offline events. The campaign raised more than $500 million from online contributions. According to the *Washington Post,* "after Alaska Gov. [and vice presidential candidate] Sarah Palin dismissed the value of community organizing in her acceptance speech at the Republican National Convention on Sept. 3 . . . Obama raised $10 million within 24 hours."[46]

The ability of social networks to rally public support has galvanized other citizens, young and old, to take advantage of social networks to increase awareness of a variety of causes. For example, filmmakers interested in social issues

"Needle in a Haystack"

In late summer 2009, an Australian tourist vacationing on the Greek island of Mykonos found a camera that obviously belonged to someone. It was filled with pictures, and although the tourist spent the next day walking around Mykonos's main village, he did not see anyone he recognized from the photos.

When the tourist returned home to Australia, he decided to see if social networking could help him reunite the camera with its owner. He started a group on Facebook, describing the situation and posting the photos. He invited his friends to join and encouraged them to spread the word. He called the group "Needle in a haystack."

He started the group on October 17, and 60 people joined the next day. Just one week later, 1,200 people had joined the group. That number rose to 18,000 by October 30 and to 60,000 by October 31. By November 2 there were 235,000 members of Needle in a haystack. Many who joined thanked him for his efforts; some had lost cameras themselves and wished someone had done the same for them.

On the morning of November 3 the search was over. Half a world away, a group in a London office recognized people in the photos, which included the camera's owner.

can join OneWorldTV and post their videos. Environmental activists can join networks such as WiserEarth or Care2. Each network seeks to connect users to communities taking action to advance causes close to their heart. However, some individuals are part of a community in which access to the Web is restricted due to security concerns. Nevertheless, many of these communities have developed ways for their members to participate in and enjoy carefully selected aspects of Web 2.0.

Social Networks for the Military

As American tweens and teens who grew up with daily Internet access reach adulthood, many of them choose to serve in the military. However, they discover that military life has a number of obligations, including keeping communications secured and restricted. This includes access to the Web.

Making Web 2.0 applications accessible to military personnel is a challenge for the armed services. For example, the U.S. Navy's Morale, Welfare and Recreation Division admits that the division has "always struggled with the challenge of getting and holding the attention of 18–25 year old service members in order to find out what they want to do in their off-duty time as well as to provide them information about available programs, events and services."[47] Consequently, the U.S. Department of Defense began a program to examine how to create social networks with the benefits of MySpace or Facebook within the confines of military security.

According to Amber Corrin, writing in *Defense Systems* magazine, one of the department's biggest challenges has been to find a way "to facilitate the open communications and transparency of social networking while still protecting networks necessary for military and government functions."[48] To that end, the department developed milBook for the U.S. Army, which debuted on a trial basis in October 2009.

Unlike a standard Web 2.0 social network, which anyone with Internet access can join, milBook is restricted to army personnel. This helps ensure that its information remains secure. And unlike other social networks, milBook has a different philosophy behind it. Justin Filler, deputy director of the army's MilTech Solutions office, says "We prefer to categorize our sites as professional networking rather than social, as the topics, information and relationships are based largely on professional similarities and common grounds."[49]

By January 2010 milBook had nearly twenty thousand users, and its success led the navy to initiate a similar endeavor. These and other government services combine Web 2.0 functionality with government services into what has become known as Government 2.0.

Government 2.0

Author William D. Eggars coined the phrase *Government 2.0* in 2005. Eggars envisioned a new generation of local, state, or national government Internet services that were citizen centered and driven by their needs. Technology and media observer Tim O'Reilly defines Government 2.0 much in the same way he defines Web 2.0, using the phrase *government as a platform.*

Government 2.0 efforts seek to bring the ease of information access available through Web 2.0 sites to national and local government information. My.BarackObama.com, created for Obama's 2008 presidential campaign, remained active after his election. The administration sees it as a way for President Obama to share information about various issues. It also serves as a way for U.S. citizens to share their thoughts about various issues and to become involved in national politics. All U.S. government agencies have some level of presence on the Web; for example, the National Park Service (NPS) started building Web sites for NPS units in the mid-1990s. Over the years, these sites have provided a means for sharing information about visitor use facilities and park management policies.

However, with these first-generation sites, users were unable to provide feedback to these sites or direct their content. Employees versed in Web 2.0 are working to make the national parks experience more interactive. One example of the successful adoption of Web 2.0 technology involves Yosemite National Park's famed Half Dome.

Web 2.0 and the Half Dome

One of the most popular attractions at Yosemite National Park in California is the mountain called Half Dome. It attracts rock climbers and casual hikers; the latter can follow a trail to the top, using the assistance of fixed cables to complete the climb. But like many other sites in national parks, the mountain is extremely popular, especially on summer weekends. In 2008 eighty-four thousand people climbed to the top of Half Dome. In 2009 up to twelve hundred people a day tried the climb, resulting in long waits and dangerous overcrowding. Park management decided to implement a permit system to limit the daily number of hikers to four hundred from May to July in 2010 and 2011 to ensure the visitors' safety and to protect the alpine ecosystem.

The park took advantage of Web 2.0 technology to spread the word about the new permit system. On January 29, 2010, at 9:08 A.M. Pacific time, the park posted this message on its Twitter feed: "In order to increase safety, permits will be required to hike Half Dome Fri-Sun + holidays this year,"[50] followed by a link to the press release. Ten minutes later, another tweet linked to a Frequently Asked Questions page about the permits.

The news spread rapidly. By 9:32 A.M. park staff was tweeting in reply to questions about the permits. Minutes later, Modern Hiker, a hiking blog for Los Angeles and southern California, and YosemiteBlog, a privately run guide to the park, posted the park's press release on their sites, and both added the news to their midmorning tweets. By lunchtime, park spokeswoman Kari Cobb had completed interviews with the Associated Press and the *San Francisco Chronicle,* and the permits were being discussed on blogs, on Twitter, and on a variety of Facebook pages. Cobb said that she and the public information officer

Be Careful What You Post

Social networks provide a valuable means for staying in touch with and meeting new friends through the Internet. Users share opinions, jokes, videos, links, and photographs. However, users need to be careful about what they post, especially if the posts show questionable activities.

An August 2009 survey conducted by CareerBuilder.com shows that people who make decisions about hiring job applicants do more than just read a resume or application. Forty-five percent of the employers said they checked the applicants' online profile. They looked at what the applicants said, what photos they posted, and the attitude the applicant seemed to have. Job candidates were turned down if they posted inappropriate photographs or information, if they had bad-mouthed a previous employer or coworkers, or if they posted content about using alcohol or drugs.

On the other hand, employers hired applicants if their social network profiles showed the candidate's creativity, their positive attitude, and their communication skills.

fielded dozens of calls from the media that day and conducted at least twenty interviews on the subject. She says,
"The word definitely got out faster using Twitter than if we
had just put out a press release."[51]

The news about changes at Half Dome is one example of
Government 2.0. Additionally, the U.S. government's clear-
inghouse Web site, USA.gov, now has a Facebook page for
more direct interaction with Web surfers needing information about government grants and benefits, disaster assistance, and federal jobs. Other nations, such as Australia
and New Zealand, have formulated their own programs of
Government 2.0. But with these changes come questions
of security and access. Government and commercial sites
both have information that needs to be kept secure, and
both need to be aware of challenges to the integrity of their
networks.

Security Concerns

Social networks are an immensely popular feature of
Web 2.0. But site administrators need to monitor the user-
driven content closely. Some Web users deliberately try to
post content that circumvents security protocols. Their
intention is often to damage the sites' servers and the computers that connect to them.

The interactive features built into Web 2.0 sites have created a variety of vulnerabilities to outside attacks. One type,
called a cross-scripting attack, enables the attacker to run
unauthorized code on the victim's browser. One result is that
the attacker can get access to the victim's login names and
passwords without the victim's knowledge. A second type of
attack, called a cross-site request forgery, occurs when the
attacker discovers a way to trick a Web site into believing
that it is exchanging data with a user who is properly logged
on, but who may actually have left the site without logging
off. In *PCWorld* magazine Robert McMillan writes, "Many
sites protect against this type of attack by automatically logging visitors off after a few minutes of inactivity, but if the
attacker could trick a victim into visiting his malicious site

just minutes after logging into, say, Bank of America's Web site, the bad guy could theoretically clean out the victim's bank account."[52]

In August 2009 Facebook was the target of such an attack. Loading an infected page would have resulted in the theft of the user's personal information. The attack was not made public until after Facebook had found and fixed the problem. The attack took advantage of a security flaw in the way information travels on the Web and the way browsers work. Each time, a browser activated a link selected by the user, as it was designed to do. The key to combating these threats is having the site's internal security recognize the source of the link as coming from or directing to an unauthorized source.

Internal design and continuous vigilance by Internet sites is only part of the battle for security and safety on Web 2.0. Users must also keep up-to-date on security threats to their computers and must practice safe surfing techniques when taking advantage of the features of social networks. However, there are individuals around the world who deliberately post distasteful and harmful content. In many cases, the targets of this content are young people, and just as often, the developers are young people too.

Cyberbullying

As more and more young people use social networks in their daily lives, many of them discover that they are being subjected to unfriendly activity. The content that targets them can taunt them about their looks or body shape. Messages can declare that no one likes them. Posts can direct death threats at them, their pets, or their family. All of these are part of what education and law enforcement officials call cyberbullying.

Cyberbullying goes much further than traditional forms of bullying that occur in school hallways and on playgrounds. When cyberbullies post on a social network, many more people learn about it than just the intended victim. Additionally, it often prompts others to join in with

Fifteen-year-old Phoebe Prince committed suicide after being bullied at school and on Facebook. Cyberbullying is becoming more common as more young people join online social networks.

their own comments about the victim. The National Crime Prevention Council reports that 58 percent of fourth through eighth graders reported having mean or cruel things said to them online, and 53 percent admitted that they had said cruel or hurtful things to others online. Forty-two percent of them maintained that they had been bullied online, and almost 60 percent have never told their parents about the incident. And teen girls are more likely to be the targets of cyberbullying than teen boys.

Far too often, the attacks have unwelcome repercussions. In the fall of 2009, fifteen-year-old Phoebe Prince moved from Ireland to the United States with her family. She enrolled as a high school freshman at a school in South Hadley, Massachusetts. Writing for the *Boston Globe,* Kevin Cullen describes Prince's life:

> She was a freshman and she had a brief fling with a senior, a football player, and for this she became the target of the [bullies], who decided then and there that Phoebe didn't know her place and that Phoebe would pay. Kids can be mean, but . . . according to students and parents . . . the name-calling, the stalking, the intimidation was relentless.[53]

In addition, Prince received similar treatment on her Facebook page and through text messages on her cell phone. One day's torment included harassment in the school library and hallways; one tormentor threw a can of soda at her. On January 14, 2010, Prince walked home from school and committed suicide. On February 22, South Hadley superintendent of schools Gus Sayer said that disciplinary action had been taken against several students who "will not be returning"[54] to the high school. In the months that followed, nine students were charged with a wide range of crimes, including statutory rape, violation of civil rights, criminal harassment, stalking, and assault by means of a dangerous weapon (the soda can).

Recognizing that cyberbullying incidents sometimes have dire results, social networks endeavor to keep lines of communication open between their users and site administrators. Facebook administrators encourage users to report cyberbullying posts and messages and to block users from posting on their pages. Bebo, which is popular with young people in Great Britain, had gained the nickname "Bully-bo" based on the large number of cyberbullying messages posted on it. Administrators reacted by adding a button to its site labeled "If you suspect it, report it!" The information on the suspected page is passed directly to the Children Exploitation and Online Protection Centre, a British program combating cyberbullying.

"I Love My Friends!"

Fortunately the vast majority of content on social networks is more constructive than destructive. For many users, their experiences have exceeded their expectations. A group of teens in Massachusetts uses MySpace to promote their hard-rock band. The lead guitarist's mother uses Facebook to tell her network of friends of the group's latest concerts, and a U.S. Air Force veteran in Colorado uses it to keep his friends updated about his wife's chemotherapy. A mother-to-be shares stories of her first pregnancy on MomsLikeMe.com. And countless individuals play a variety of interactive games, making new friends from around the world.

One Facebook user, who joined in 2009, discovered that the social network lets her keep up with current friends and family, but it also put her back in touch with so many friends from her past. She says, "I've spent more time on the computer than all the other years of my computer time added up . . . yikes. . . . I'm more the nature girl . . . but I LOVE MY FRIENDS!"[55] The evolving world of Web 2.0 presents new and different opportunities for people to reconnect with old friends and connect with new ones. It gives them a chance to share new things in their lives. In addition, it gives a segment of the population a new outlet for demonstrating their creativity. And the user-driven nature of Web 2.0 presents them with a potential audience of millions.

CHAPTER 4

Mashing, Memes, and More

S ocial networking requires no special software or computer skills beyond a desktop or laptop with an Internet connection. However, other Web 2.0 applications provide outlets for those with other talents, such as photographers, graphic artists, musicians, and designers. These individuals have discovered that Web 2.0 presents them with a variety of opportunities. They can share their efforts beyond the confines of their home or studio and have their efforts seen and shared by more than just friends and customers. Sometimes, their creativity is shared and experienced by potentially millions of Internet users.

The *Hampster Dance*

In the early days of the Internet, Canadian art student Deidre LaCarte was competing with a friend to see whose Web site could generate the most traffic. She used her pet hamster, Hampton, as the inspiration for her site, which she called Hampton's Hamster House. She used four animated images of rodents and other animals, repeated in a line dozens of times, and linked it with a nine-second loop of music. LaCarte called the animation *Hampster Dance*, and Hampton's Hamster House became one of the first truly phenomenal Internet animation sites.

From its debut in August 1998 until January 1999, the site only recorded only a few hits a day. But then suddenly, the site jumped from an average of four hits a day to more than fifteen thousand. News of the site's simple yet hypnotically entertaining animation had spread not only via word of mouth, but through e-mail links and early blogs. The *Hampster Dance* was even used in a commercial for Internet service provider Earthlink.

Other animated dances followed, trying to build on LaCarte's success. Variations featured then–U.S. vice president Dan Quayle and PEZ candy dispensers. But Hampton's Hamster House paved the way for what was to come in the world of entertainment on the Internet.

JibJab

In 1999 brothers Greg and Evan Spiridelis combined computer equipment, a dial-up Internet connection, and a dream to create entertainment recognized around the world into a company they called JibJab. Their animation techniques mashed up photos of celebrities, politicians, and people in the news with animated bodies and music to create parodies and social commentaries.

JibJab attracted widespread attention during the 2004 U.S. presidential campaign when its Flash video featuring caricatures of candidates George W. Bush and John Kerry singing "This Land Is Your Land" was shown on a variety of national news broadcasts and on the late-night television show *The Tonight Show with Jay Leno*. The video was viewed more than 80 million times online, on every continent, and was even uploaded to the International Space Station.

Since the 2004 success of *This Land*, JibJab has premiered ten original videos on *The Tonight Show*, including a variety of political parodies and "year-in-review" musical films. JibJab's Web 2.0 site also invites users to upload friends' and family's faces to create their own short films and electronic greeting cards.

Early Web Music and Video

The world of entertainment often appeals to one or more of the senses, such as sight and sound. On the early Internet, entertainment was usually only sight related. But individuals with artistic minds realized that the Internet held great potential as an outlet for their creativity. However, sharing art, music, and video on Web 1.0 was difficult. Some bands and their fans created Web sites with recordings and videos available as downloadable links, and some pioneering individuals created personal pages with embedded homemade films. Some of these videos were quite impressive; their intricate editing and soundtracks demonstrated true dedication to the art form. But each site was purely a Web 1.0 experience.

When traditional media outlets, such as television stations, began to create Web 2.0 sites, they included videos of news stories. Users could link to them through their social networks or through microblog sites, such as Digg or reddit. Aspiring filmmakers and musicians used MySpace to post documentaries and concert videos. But it fell to three innovators to change music and video on the Web. These former PayPal employees wanted to make sharing videos as easy as attaching a file to an e-mail.

BITS & BYTES

20

Hours of video posted to YouTube every minute, every day

YouTube

In the winter of 2005, three former employees of the online payment site PayPal were trying to figure out a way to make sharing videos easier on the Web. Chad Hurley, Steve Chen, and Jawed Karim created a site they called YouTube, which debuted in a limited, six-month trial version in May 2005. During its first two months, YouTube ran a contest, giving away an iPod Nano to a random member each day. Members got points for posting videos and inviting friends, among other tasks. It got YouTube noticed among their target audience: teens, college students, hobbyists, and filmmakers. As one blogger put it, "after all, if you knew you had a chance

Two of the founders of YouTube, Chad Hurley (left) and Steve Chen created the site in order to make sharing videos easier on the Web. The site grew so quickly that within a little more than a year YouTube was purchased by Google for $1.65 billion.

[of] winning a $250 iPod Nano just by signing up and posting that Uncle Bob's funny biking incident clip you've had on your hard-drive for the past few years, wouldn't you?"[56]

The YouTube developers soon discovered that the videos that were being uploaded were from a wide variety of sources and covered an amazing range of topics. According to John Cloud, who profiled YouTube's founders for *Time* magazine in 2006, "many kids were linking to YouTube from their MySpace pages, and YouTube's growth piggybacked on MySpace's."[57] By the end of the year, YouTube was also attracting advertisers and investors. More money came in as YouTube continued to grow; by the summer of 2006, it was the fifth most popular site on the Web. A July 2006 survey showed 100 million video clips were being viewed daily, and 65,000 were being uploaded every twenty-four hours. YouTube's growth led Google to purchase it in October 2006 for $1.65 billion.

The growth of YouTube was mimicked by the growth of other Web 2.0 sites, such as Facebook and Twitter. Visitors to YouTube found interesting videos and added links to them on their social network pages, driving more traffic to YouTube. By 2010 twenty hours of videos were being uploaded to

POPULAR WEB SITES 2.0 (MAY2010)

Rank	Web site	Category	Est. Unique Monthly Visitor
1	Facebook	social networking	250,000,000
2	YouTube	video	175,000,000
3	Wikipedia	reference /wiki*	125,000,000
4	MySpace	social networking	122,000,000
5	Blogger	blogging	121,000,000
6	craigslist	social networking/ commerce	90,000,000
7	WordPress	blogging	89,500,000
8	Twitter	micro-blogging/ social networking	80,500,000
9	flickr	social media (photos)	79,000,000
10	IMDB (International Movie Database)	reference	60,000,000
11	photobucket	social media (photos)	55,000,000
12	digg	social news	45,000,000
13	eHow	reference	43,000,000
14	TypePad	blogging	26,000,000
15	HubPages	blogging	24,500,000

Data: Select information from "Top 15 Most Popular Web 2.0 Websites, May 2010." eBizMBA. Available from http://www.ebizmba.com/articles/web-2.0-websites. And "Top 20 Most Popular Social Networking Sites." Available from http://www.ebizma.com/articles/social-networking-websites.

YouTube every minute of every day, and daily viewers numbered in the hundreds of millions. It is, therefore, not surprising that budding filmmakers and other aspiring artists choose to share their work on the site.

"Broadcast Yourself"

YouTube's slogan, "Broadcast Yourself," has inspired people to promote their creative side. Some videos are made by one person with a camera, intending to document an important family milestone. For example, there are more than ten thousand videos of a baby taking his or her first steps. Others catch important events, such as weather phenomena or natural disasters; there are over fourteen thousand videos showing tornadoes from 2009.

Other videos took more time and effort to complete. A wedding ceremony and reception may last several hours before the last guest leaves; a filmmaker can edit the full-length video into four or five minutes of highlights for family and friends to share. A proud parent may record an entire sporting event and edit out everything not involving his or her child, thereby compiling the son's or daughter's goals in soccer or hockey.

In addition, musicians use video-sharing sites to promote their performances. Well-edited videos can highlight the talents of each musician in a group as well as document the overall sound. Such efforts usually require more than one camera and multiple microphones. Following the innovative efforts of club DJs whose knowledge of various album or CD tracks enabled them to create new and seamless flows of music, Web 2.0 innovators began to discover that they could mix two or more parts of separate programs or Web sites to create something new.

Mash It Up

In the world of the Web, a mixture of two or more features to create a new one is called a mashup. A mashup can combine art with music, music with music, music with video, information with information, or any two or more services that the developer can imagine. The data is combined and remixed to create an entirely new piece of art or an innovative service that conveys information as never before.

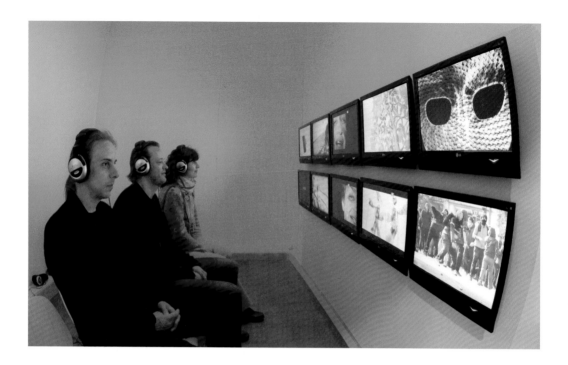

The key to creating a mashup is a feature of software called an application programming interface (API). An API enables one piece of software to interact with other software. When a developer creates a program, he or she has to consider how the program will interact with other programs. For example, in order to cut and paste text from a Web page into a word processing program, the program running the Web page and the computer's word processor need to interact. Otherwise, the pasted information will be indecipherable. Some companies choose to keep their APIs private; others release them to the public in order to facilitate outside interests to create new software that will interact with theirs.

The Web site ProgrammableWeb.com maintains a catalog of public APIs, as well as a list of most-used and newly released APIs. They also have lists of mashups by category, such as "Celebrity," "Sports," and "Maps." Each mashup is accompanied by the APIs used to construct it and the mashup's URL. Some are worldwide in scope; others are local. For

By mashing up art, music, and video an artist created this video installation titled Music From The Masses *on display in a German gallery. Combining and remixing data can create an entirely new piece of art or an innovative service that conveys information as never before.*

example, in the Sports category a runner can find a mashup that shows the route and elevations along the way of the Austin, Texas, marathon; in the Maps category, amateur and professional geologists can track earthquakes recorded globally every week.

Commercial enterprises have discovered that mashups can streamline information gathering and processing, and therefore can save time, effort, and money. James Niccolai, writing in *PCWorld* magazine, relates one success story:

> Great Lakes Educational Loan Services used an external e-signature service from DocuSign to help it deal with the flood of loan requests it gets [in the spring] each year. It combined the service with its loan application system on its Web site. In the first two months, 80 percent of its 72,000 applicants used e-signatures, which cut its costs in this area by 75 percent.[58]

As mashups have become more popular, Web 2.0 heavyweights, such as Amazon, Google, and Facebook, have released their APIs for developers to use. In addition, a number of government-related APIs are available for mashing, from U.S. congressional speech data to documents from the Dutch Parliament. Mashers then create services that combine traffic data, crime statistics, and houses for sale with APIs from Google Maps, used car ads with APIs from eBay, and wildlife photograph collections with APIs from Flickr. While YouTube makes it easy to post videos to its site, YouTube's publicly available API enables performers to reach an even wider audience. The API enables Web designers to mashup YouTube's video player on their sites to display as many videos as they wish. And with the API from Facebook, they can mashup fan pages with photos, videos, and downloadable songs.

But there are other creative efforts that also come under the definition of *mashup*. These endeavors mix two songs or videos together to create something new, or mix songs with new video, and they are helping to expand the boundaries of entertainment.

Music Mashups

Music mashups have become a popular entertainment genre. They have come a considerable distance from the first recordings by DJs synchronizing the beats and rhythms of two songs on adjacent turntables and then playing tracks at the same time. Today the Web has a variety of sites featuring mashups of seemingly incongruous artists, such as 1960s heavy metal icons Iron Butterfly and 1980s synth-pop group New Order or 1990s grunge pioneers Nirvana with performer Lady Gaga.

Other mashup DJs work directly with artists. Jordan Roseman, who goes by the nickname DJ Earworm, has worked with a variety of artists to mash their music into "greatest hits" tracks, including Grammy Award winner Annie Lennox and reggae-fusion artist Sean Kingston. The alternative-rock band Maroon 5 gave him access to the digital recordings of all their songs, giving DJ Earworm great freedom to create mashups. He explains,

> I could go in and grab whatever instrument or vocal I wanted. This is the first time I've gotten such a depth of data to work with. As I picked apart the recording sessions, the thing that really stood out to me was the level of musicianship buried in the many layers. What sounded like a simple guitar riff was actually made up of many guitars, carefully layered and ordered to get just the right tone. Background vocals revealed themselves to be beautiful melodies in their own right. [The mashup] has an electro house club feel. I added some guitars from "Goodnight Goodnight," "This Love," and "Makes Me Wonder," and brought in the piano from "She Will be Loved."[59]

DJ Earworm started making mashups in 2003 as a hobby after graduating from the University of Illinois with a degree in computer science and music theory. He shared his tapes with DJ Adrian, a friend who was working at the first mashup club in San Francisco. He says that Adrian "got me to put them online and then they just started to take off."[60] His end-of-the-year compilations, called "The United State of Pop," mash the top twenty-five songs of the year into about six minutes. The tracks are extremely popular; M. Tye Comer, executive director of Billboard.com, says DJ Earworm is "blowing up right now," believing that his success reflects how people find information today. "People are more apt to discover things online, and I think the time was right for his talent and his technique to be consumed. I think the stars aligned [in his favor]."[61]

DJ Earworm's success seems to go hand in hand with his increased proficiency at his craft. His 2009-in-review mashup quickly went viral in early 2010; in other words, it became extremely popular in a short period of time. Web 2.0 applications make spreading the word about a favorite video a relatively easy task; a user can post a link to it on their social network page, blog about it, tweet about it, or vote for it on a news site. And viral videos have made some people Internet stars virtually overnight.

Viral Videos

There is no guarantee that today's viral video will still be popular in the future. Because the Web is constantly changing, a wildly popular video can be replaced by something new tomorrow. But there are a number of viral videos that have withstood the test of time, remaining popular years after they were first seen. One of these is *The Evolution of Dance*, featuring Judson Laipply, an inspirational speaker and comedian based in Cleveland, Ohio. In this six-minute video, Laipply performs snippets of popular dances since the 1950s to a musical montage. It is a simple video; one camera focuses on Laipply on a stage. Part of the video's appeal is the pure physicality of it, as Laipply moves from one dance style to another with rapid-fire intensity. Another part is the audience's reaction, as they whoop and holler in recognition of a song, the dance, or both. This video has been viewed nearly 150 million times since it was posted in 2006.

Other videos have generated viral attention and then seemingly just as quickly fallen out of favor. One such series

Judson Laipply, seen posing with the Cleveland skyline in the background, created one of the most popular viral videos of all time. His "The Evolution of Dance" video has been viewed more than 150 million times since 2006.

of videos, shot by a single Webcam, appeared in the spring of 2006. Each featured a young woman who called herself Bree, and each was posted under the screen name lonelygirl15. A new video appeared every few days and they attracted a worldwide following; several topped six hundred thousand views each. In the *Los Angeles Times* Richard Rushfield and Claire Hoffman write,

> Lonelygirl15 appears to be an innocent, home-schooled 16-year-old, pouring her heart out for her video camera in the privacy of her bedroom. But since May, her brief posts on the video-sharing site YouTube and the social networking hub MySpace have launched a Web mystery eagerly followed by her million-plus viewers: Who is this sheltered ingénue who calls herself "Bree," and is she in some sort of danger—or, worse, the tool of some giant marketing machine?[62]

Shortly after the *Los Angeles Times* article appeared, "Bree" was exposed as an actress named Jennifer Rose, and the videos were revealed to be a hoax as part of a fictional story. Today a search for "lonelygirl15" on YouTube generates far more videos in reaction to Bree's story than the actual videos themselves.

Other viral videos are truly professional productions, featuring sophisticated editing, sets, extras, and talented performers. They connect with viewers in a variety of ways, such as the common emotions of frustration and loss. One of these is *United Breaks Guitars,* by Canadian musician Dave Carroll. In 2008 Carroll and his band, Sons of Maxwell, flew on United Airlines to Nebraska to perform some concerts; however, while changing planes in Chicago, Illinois, Carroll's thirty-five-hundred-dollar Taylor guitar was damaged by United Airlines baggage handlers. Carroll spent a year phoning and e-mailing the airline, trying to get compensation, to no avail. His frustration led him to compose the song "United Breaks Guitars," which recounts his ordeal. He posted a video of himself singing the song on YouTube on July 6, 2009, and it went viral within the week. On July 10, in an interview on the television show *The Early Show,* Carroll said when he went to bed on the night he posted the video, it had had six hits, "and I was

The Saga of "Balloon Boy"

On October 15, 2009, television, radio, and Web news services around the world followed a developing story in Colorado. A homemade hot air balloon was streaking across the countryside near Fort Collins. According to many reports, the balloon owner's six-year-old son, Falcon Heene, was trapped inside. National Guard and television station helicopters tracked it across the countryside, and emergency personnel followed it from the ground. When the balloon finally landed, it was empty. Instead, Falcon had been hiding at home the entire afternoon.

Falcon was quickly dubbed "Balloon Boy," and his story went viral. "Balloon Boy" came from a tweet by television station KUSA while the balloon was in flight. Web 2.0 users around the world watched the drama unfold on their computers or cell phones and posted reactions throughout the balloon's flight.

The story continued to resonate across the Internet even after Falcon was found safe and sound. An investigation by authorities found that the balloon flight was a publicity stunt designed by Falcon's parents. They were hoping to get their own reality TV show. The stunt resulted in criminal proceedings, fines, and jail time for both parents.

impressed by that number at that time. Topping out at over a million now is pretty overwhelming in three days."[63] That same day, Carroll expressed his gratitude in another video, saying the number of views of his song was "more than I ever could have hoped."[64]

What Makes a Video Viral?

Dave Carroll did not set out to create a viral video, yet within ten days *United Breaks Guitars* had more than 10 million views worldwide. Web 2.0 observers and social experts agree that three important factors contribute to making a video popular enough to go viral. First, videos that show something never seen before are very likely to generate word-of-mouth traffic. In Web 2.0 terms, of course, that means massive sharing through social networking, through microblog references, and through clicks on the site hosting the video. One example is the performance of singer Susan Boyle on the British television show *Britain's Got Talent* in April 2009, in which she brought the audience to its feet with her stunningly glorious singing voice. A copy of her performance posted online drew an estimated 100 million views in the first few weeks.

Secondly, short videos are generally more likely to go viral than longer ones. Warren Zenna and Max Rosen of Indigo Productions in New York City point out that "most successful viral videos are short. Four minutes is considered roughly equivalent to "Gone with the Wind" [which runs nearly 4 hours]. Many viral videos are under 30 seconds—showing nothing more than a clip from a crazy car accident or a wacky incident with a pet."[65]

Lastly, the video should make people laugh. Although humor is very subjective—what one person finds funny is not funny to another—some things seem to connect with most viewers. Making light of a bad situation, as Dave Carroll did with *United Breaks Guitars,* or demonstrating an unexpected talent,

BITS & BYTES
150,000
Number of hits the *Pants on the Ground* video received in its first twelve hours on the Web

as Jason Laipply did with *Evolution of Dance,* will get people smiling and laughing.

Sometimes responding to a viral video can also lead to viral status. In the summer of 2009, a video called *Jill and Kevin's Big Day* (also called *JK Wedding Entrance Dance*) rocketed onto the viral video scene. People's response was "wow!" and it made them laugh. Almost a year after its posting, it was still in YouTube's top ten among entertainment videos. In August Indigo Productions filmed a parody of it, called *JK Divorce Entrance Dance;* in six weeks it had more than 10 million views. Both the original and the parody generated interest in the traditional media as well as the Internet, turning the Entrance Dance videos into a "meme."

American Idol contestant Larry Platt's audition where he sang his song Pants on the Ground *quickly became a meme on the Web. Less than two months after the audition aired on January 13, 2010, YouTube had more than 20,000 videos relating to it.*

Memes

A meme is more than just one viral video or one rapidly spreading image or phrase found on the Web. Instead, a meme is best defined as an idea or a topic, which gets spread and expanded upon by additional creative minds online. Jennifer Van Grove, writing for the Web site Mashable, defines a meme as content that "spreads from person to person in a viral manner."[66] Her Mashable colleagues Dan Zarella and Alison Driscoll call it "an idea that you can't help sharing with your friends."[67]

Before Web 2.0, sharing with your friends meant attaching an image, video, or link to an e-mail, or perhaps posting it on a blog, hoping people would read it. Some Web observers consider the 1990s-era *Hampster Dance* the first Internet meme, as it gave birth to a large number of imitators, which were spread largely by e-mail. But with

Web 2.0, and the wider variety of sharing options, memes spread faster than ever before. And with the wide availability of Web-based photo- and video-editing software, artistic minds can develop and post their creations faster than ever before.

One example of the speed at which a meme can develop is Larry Platt's performance on the television show *American Idol.* He sang a song that he wrote, called "Pants on the Ground." The broadcast aired on television on January 13, 2010, and the first YouTube video (a clip from the show posted by Fox Television) received 150,000 hits in its first twelve hours. Comic Jimmy Fallon performed the song on his late-night television show two nights later, impersonating rock star Neil Young. "Pants on the Ground" quickly became a meme; less than two months later, YouTube had over twenty

I Can Has Cheezburger

Internet memes based on ideas or phrases can also generate viral attention. The Web site "I Can Has Cheezburger" has thousands of photos of cats doing a wide variety of activities, such as napping, climbing, and investigating. People have added captions that supposedly portray the cat's thoughts, such as the photo of a cat relaxing in front of a fire in a fireplace supposedly thinking "another day successfully wasted." The I Can Has Cheezburger meme is so successful that it led to a theater production called *I Can Has Cheezburger: The MusicLOL!* that ran during the 2009 FringeNYC festival in New York City.

Barb Dybwad of Mashable notes that there is another indicator of when a meme is a hit. She writes, "You know your Internet meme has hit the big time when other Internet memes spring up to spoof it." One spoof is the Web site AverageCats, in which users can also find captioned photos of cats being cats, but the captions demonstrate that the cats are merely being cats. There are no plots to take revenge on dogs and no ulterior motives behind napping on a closed laptop.

I Can Has Cheezburger, "Another Day," March 8, 2010, http://icanhascheezburger.com/2010/03/08/funny-pictures-day-successfuly-wasted.

Barb Dybwad, "AverageCats Celebrates Mediocrity with LOLcats Parody," Mashable, October 8, 2009, http://mashable.com/2009/10/08/averagecats.

thousand videos related to it, including remixes, mashups, and additional parodies.

One long-lasting Web meme is the Internet equivalent of a practical joke. Taking advantage of intense interest in a particular person or event, an individual will post a link to a video that relates to the topic at hand. But when a user clicks on the link, quite a different video appears, along with a message saying that the user has been "Rickrolled."

Rickrolling

Unlike other deliberately misleading links on the Internet, "Rickroll" pages are merely a bait and switch. The video that appears is of 1980s artist Rick Astley performing his 1987 hit song, "Never Gonna Give You Up." The first-known instance of Rickrolling occurred in May 2007, on the video game message board of the 4chan Web site. A link that supposedly led a reader to a trailer for the upcoming video game Grand Theft Auto IV instead led to the Astley video, along with the caption, "You've been Rickrolled!"

Within a year, the video, or pieces of it, were popping up across the Web. Sometimes Astley's song began at the start of the video; in other cases, pranksters inserted it thirty seconds or so into the seemingly normal video. The practice had become so widespread that it became the subject of an April 2008 poll by SurveyUSA. Their findings suggest that "at least 18 million Americans have been on the receiving end of the prank," but the company also notes that "this is likely an underestimation, as the poll was unable to include those under the age of 18."[68]

For his part, Rick Astley does not mind being associated with an Internet prank. In an interview with the *Los Angeles Times,* he says, "I think it's just one of those odd things where something gets picked up and people run with it. But that's what's brilliant about the Internet."[69] Other artists, however, are not so generous. Web sites are often obliged to remove artistic creations that use content illegally, raising questions of copyrights and fair use.

Fair Use or Infringement?

Any artistic creation is subject to copyright law. This law protects any new creation, whether it is a photograph, a painting or drawing, or a composition of music or writing, in when and how it can be used or reproduced. The artist or author can protest when someone has used all or part of his or her work without permission. It does not matter if the work is intended for sale or not.

Filmmakers, for example, must obtain an artist's permission for any music they use in their films. Mashup artists work similarly; DJ Earworm makes it clear that he does not wish to infringe on an artist's copyrights. He feels that it is important to work with the artist if there is a feeling of infringement. He says, "I think if you transform [the song] enough it's ok. I have always cooperated in the theoretical possibility that someone would want me to take it down. But mostly people want me to help them so it is kind of the opposite of what you may think. People are for it."[70]

He points out that he cannot legally sell the mashups he creates, unless he is under contract with an artist.

Singer Kanye West's interruption of Taylor Swift's acceptance speech during the 2009 MTV Video Music Awards quickly became a meme which included his image and the phrase "Ima let you finish" pasted onto a variety of videos and images across the Web.

Otherwise, the mashups he creates by sampling other people's work are free, and in the words of CNN reporter Jo Piazza, "he is truly just creating mashups for the love of the music."[71]

The love of the music is at the heart of a concept of copyright law called fair use. According Piazza, "mashup artists are usually able to skirt copyright laws under the 'fair use' doctrine."[72] In other words, if the mashups are not for sale, but for entertainment purposes only, there is no copyright infringement. The question of what constitutes fair use hangs over the growing realms of mashups and memes. According to the U.S. Copyright Office, "the distinction between fair use and infringement may be unclear and not easily defined. There is no specific number of words, lines, or notes that may safely be taken without permission."[73] Therefore, the masher who uses a rhythm line from two artists may find that one artist claims infringement and the other does not.

An entire meme may raise questions of fair use. The snowy owl in the "O RLY?" meme (short for the sarcastic phrase, "Oh, really?") is a copyrighted photo by nature photographer John White. He uploaded it to a newsgroup Web site in 2001, but the owl's image was later cropped onto a new background and the caption "O RLY?" inserted. It has been reproduced countless times without White's permission. Following singer Kanye West's interruption of singer Taylor Swift's acceptance speech at the 2009 Video Music Awards, his phrase "Ima let you finish" and his image became a meme. He and the phrase were pasted onto a wide range of images and videos, including Leonardo da Vinci's *The Last Supper*, a screen grab from a Super Mario Brothers video game, and President Obama's 2009 State of the Union address. And each was done without West's permission or the permission of the various organizations holding copyrights to the art.

Unquestionably Web 2.0 has allowed countless artists of all types of media to share their creations worldwide. Some post their work in order to make money. Others do so hoping that someone who notices their work will pay them to create more. But many more are like DJ Earworm. Their interests are not in making money; they are crafting art for the pure joy of it. However idealistic their actions are, the reality is that the Internet has become a business. As Web 2.0 sites grow in users and in popularity, their owners and developers need to generate revenue if they are to continue to offer their services. Simply put, in order to stay in business and to secure their future, these sites need to make money. That is the reality of the Internet today, and it may be the reality of the Internet in the future as it moves beyond Web 2.0.

CHAPTER 5

Beyond Web 2.0

Today the Internet seems to be everywhere. Users can access it on computers in homes and offices, on laptops in airports and classrooms, and on cell phones in countless locations. Web 2.0 applications enable users to share information, observations, and actions from almost anywhere and from a variety of devices.

But it is important to remember that people are at the heart of the Internet, not machines. Machines make the Web possible, but it is people who create them and use them. Around the world, many people analyze the Internet, examining trends and fads. Some analysts take a long-term view, studying the present to imagine what the Web will look like in the years to come. Others take a short-term view, envisioning ways for companies and services to survive and thrive right now.

The Business Side of Web 2.0

Many of the entrepreneurs who developed Web 2.0 applications were unfamiliar with the business of business. They were often less interested in making money than they were in trying to get as many hits on their sites as possible. They started their services and, in some cases, ran them for many years, without the benefit of a plan for the business, called a business model. A business model requires a company's executives to examine

An Internet Pioneer Looks Forward . . . from 1999

Robert W. Taylor is one of the unsung heroes of the Internet. As head of the Department of Defense's Advanced Research Projects Agency (ARPA) in 1962, he hired J.C.R. Licklider and secured funding for the development of the ARPANET. He also worked with Xerox Corporation, contributing to the development of the personal computer.

In 1999 the retired Taylor was interviewed by journalist John Markoff for the *New York Times*. Taylor said that he envisioned that the coming broadband networks would couple with a wearable device "that will record in full color and sound everything that you see or point your head at, or, depending on how many of them you have, everything that's around you. And share it. Every waking and sleeping moment in your life will be recorded. And you will be able to store and retrieve it and do what you will with it." He also expressed concern for the growing popularity of the Internet, saying, "I want the Internet to become a right, not a privilege. I think we need a driver's license to allow you to use the Internet, much like you drive on the road today. If you misbehave on the road, you get your license taken away."

Quoted in John Markoff, "An Internet Pioneer Ponders the Next Revolution," *New York Times*, December 20, 1999, http://partners.nytimes.com/library/tech/99/12/biztech/articles/122099outlook-bobb.html.

the company's strengths and weaknesses and the market it targets. It requires executives to plan for the company's future and to determine how to raise money.

Most companies need money to start operating. Money allows them to hire employees, to buy equipment, and to buy or rent office space. But the popular image of Web 2.0 companies is different. It depicts entrepreneurs like Shawn Fanning of Napster or Mark Zuckerberg of Facebook sitting alone with a laptop, creating code and making a dream come to life. It seems that money comes into the picture only after the site becomes popular. As traffic begins to overload the hosting servers, the original developers need an infusion of cash quickly.

Consequently many of these companies work with venture capitalists, investors who give money to the company for short-term use in exchange for future repayment, such as

As of August 2010 Facebook founder Mark Zuckerberg had declined all offers to buy the popular Web site. Instead the site stays in business by generating revenue in a variety of ways such as virtual gifts, virtual goods, and online games.

stock shares. For example, venture capitalists invested millions of dollars in the social network Friendster, believing its early success was a promise of even larger, future accomplishments. When Friendster was surpassed by MySpace, Friendster was forced to raise more and more venture capital to stay competitive before largely giving up on the American market. Today Friendster remains a social network, with its services most popular in Asia.

Selling the Business of Web 2.0

Friendster founder Jonathan Abrams is no longer involved with the company. He was replaced as the company's chief executive in 2004, a year after he rejected a $30 million offer for the company from Google. MySpace, on the other hand, agreed to be purchased in July 2005, less than two years after its debut, for $540 million by News Corporation, which is run by media mogul Rupert Murdoch.

INTERNET ADVERTISING REVENUE COMPARED TO OTHER MEDIA OUTLETS

Every year, advertisers spend billions of dollars to market their products through a variety of media sources. Traditionally, television and print media outlets have dominated the world of advertising sales. Recently, many Web 2.0 sites, such as YouTube, have begun selling advertising spots and as a result Internet advertising revenue has skyrocketed.

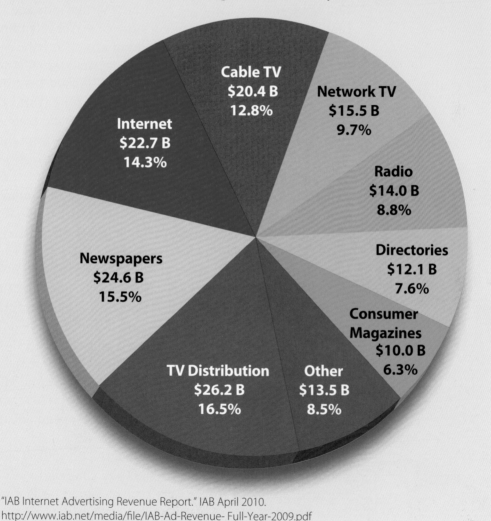

"IAB Internet Advertising Revenue Report." IAB April 2010.
http://www.iab.net/media/file/IAB-Ad-Revenue- Full-Year-2009.pdf

With Facebook's meteoric rise, business experts have wondered if it has a business model and if it is for sale. In a 2008 interview with a German business magazine, Facebook's Mark Zuckerberg said, "In three years from now we have to figure out what the optimum [business] model is. But that is not our primary focus today."[74] He also noted that he had received offers to buy Facebook, but had declined all of them. Instead, Facebook works to stay in business by generating revenue in a variety of ways beyond venture capital.

For Facebook and many other social networks, the current hot trend in generating revenue is virtual gifts and virtual goods. Instead of visiting a store or a Web site to buy a bouquet of real flowers or a balloon arrangement, social network members can choose to send a virtual gift of flowers or balloons instead for a small fee. Additionally, members who play online games, such as FarmVille or Café World, can buy virtual goods and equipment online to expand their virtual world. The money adds up quickly; revenue from these items on Facebook, MySpace, and other social networks hit $1 billion in 2009.

For the founders of another Web 2.0 hallmark, YouTube, joining a larger company was the best way to stay afloat. In November 2006, they accepted a purchase offer from Google for $1.65 billion. Founders Chad Hurley and Steve Chen remain at the company (the third founder, Jawed Karim, left in 2007), Google brought expertise that has helped YouTube grow both in popularity and in revenue. According to *Forbes* magazine writers Quentin Hardy and Evan Hessel, "Google grows by making the Web bigger and putting ads in all the new places. It's doing that at YouTube, with a few twists. An ad on the YouTube home page, something Chad Hurley experimented with before Google bought YouTube, now costs $175,000 a day, plus a commitment to spend $50,000 more in ads on Google or YouTube."[75]

Some advertisers buy small ads that roll up while a video plays; others choose to buy a YouTube channel to advertise their products. Advertisers such as Universal Pictures, Subaru, and Old Spice buy channels at $200,000 apiece and upload videos for all to see. One expert estimated that the ads will generate more than $900 million in 2010.

However, many technology and business observers agree that the business of Web 2.0 is no longer confined to users connecting with friends, playing games, or watching videos while sitting at a keyboard. For them, the future of the Internet is in devices that people carry in their pockets.

Calling Web 2.0

Computers are not the only late-twentieth-century technology that has become increasingly smaller and more powerful with each passing year. The cell phone is now more than just an instrument for making calls or sending texts. Millions of users purchase phones that can access the Internet.

The expansion of high-speed data connections across the United States throughout the start of the twenty-first century was accompanied by new cell phone models with Internet capabilities called smartphones. Models in Apple's iPhone and Research In Motion's BlackBerry product lines provide users with the ability to perform many of the traditional tasks found on desktop computers, such as e-mailing and surfing the Web. After Apple released its application programming interface (API), developers created a wide variety of applications for the phone, such as for playing games or finding stores. Some were available for free, others for a small fee. For example, one iPhone user purchased an application from the American Red Cross on first aid for $3.99, and it later helped save his life. Dan Woolley, a film producer from Colorado, was trapped when his hotel in Haiti collapsed during an earthquake in January 2010. According to Todd Wright of NBC Miami,

> Woolley used the light from his iPhone to show him his injuries and diagnosed it properly as a broken foot. Then, he used the instructions from the app [application] to treat the excessive bleeding from cuts on his legs and the back of his head. Woolley used his shirt to tie off the three-inch gash that was opened on his leg and a sock to bandage the back of his head. He said he also looked up ways to stop from going into shock.[76]

Most smartphone users will likely not find themselves in such life-threatening circumstances. But Woolley's story made the Red Cross application very popular in the weeks that followed.

Apple and its associated developers are not the only ones in the smartphone application game. Web 2.0 innovator Google entered the competition with the introduction of the Android operating system. Tech-savvy owners and developers can create applications for Android-powered phones to interface

Petabytes, Exabytes, Zettabytes, and Yottabytes

The tremendous rise in Web-based video, as well as the growth of smartphones that access the Internet has led to exponential growth in traffic across the Internet. For example, Cisco Systems, which generates an annual report that charts changes in the Internet, estimates that by 2013, video will comprise 90 percent of all Internet traffic. This is forcing those who track Internet traffic to talk about the present and future states of the Web in new terms.

Doug Webster works for Cisco Systems. He says, "When we started releasing data publicly, we measured it in petabytes of traffic. Then a couple of years ago we had to start measuring them in zettabytes, and now we're measuring them in what we call yottabytes."

One petabyte equals 1 million gigabytes. One zettabyte is 1 million petabytes, and 1 yottabyte is 1,000 zettabytes. Cisco's studies say that the amount of data that crossed the Internet from its inception through 2009 was 150 exabytes, where 1 exabyte equals 1,000 petabytes. By comparison, the studies estimate that in 2010 alone, total traffic across the Web will equal 175 exabytes.

Quoted in John Markoff, "Scientists Strive to Map the Shape-Shifting Web," *New York Times*, March 1, 2010.

with Web 2.0 services, such as Twitter and Facebook. Additionally, Android-powered phones run a variety of Web-based Google applications. Users can upload videos directly to YouTube, access Google Maps Navigation, or access their Google Gmail e-mail account, all without having to worry about memory, storage, or software, because they are working in "the cloud."

Cloud Computing

One of the frontiers of Web 2.0 is called cloud computing. E-mail users who have accounts with Yahoo! or Gmail may be familiar with the concept of "the cloud" without knowing it: They are using software running on other computers. In fact, many of Web 2.0's functions are based on cloud computing. Videos on YouTube, television programs on Hulu, or full-length movies on Netflix reside on the company's servers. Provided that a Web surfer's computer is properly equipped, users can access these videos in "the cloud" without having to download them, which takes up valuable time and hard drive space. For example, installing Adobe's free Flash Player enables Web surfers to enjoy videos from YouTube, Hulu, Google Video, and many Web news outlets. Similarly, Facebook and Flickr

Downloading Adobe Flash Player allows Web surfers to access videos in "the cloud" without having to download the videos and take up valuable time and hard drive space on their computers.

members can see videos by their friends and colleagues replayed in Flash.

One of the other advantages of cloud computing is that users are freed from the need to keep programs up-to-date. The sites hosting the software take care of that. For example, Microsoft regularly issues updates to address security or programming issues for its Office programs, such as Word and Excel, requiring personal computer users to download large files and install fixes. Google has a suite of programs in the cloud that perform similar functions, so the user does not need to install software or updates.

However, the cloud holds far more potential than just storing e-mail, photos, and documents. Enterprising companies offer a variety of services in the cloud that otherwise would have resided on a local server or desktop. One pioneer in this world is Salesforce, which since 1999 has offered cloud-based customer relationship management services, such as accounting data, sales contacts, and marketing data. According to Chris Kanaracus of *PCWorld* magazine, Salesforce's new small business service enables clients to "stock each of their contact pages with a variety of information, such as upcoming meetings, shared documents and connections to the contact's Twitter feed and LinkedIn profile."[77]

To access all that information, a Salesforce client merely opens a browser and logs on to his or her account. The data remains on Salesforce's servers, and the client is freed from having to upgrade software, perform hard drive maintenance, and perform backups.

For information and business technology author Nicholas Carr says cloud-based services are the future of the Web. He envisions a time when personal computers may become obsolete, replaced by "thin clients," a machine that is little more than a monitor connected to the Internet. Carr writes,

> Today, it's hard to imagine computer owners in the United States and other developed countries abandoning their PCs for thin clients. Many of us, after all, have dozens or even hundreds of gigabytes of data on our own personal hard drives, including hefty music

and video files. But once [cloud computing] services mature, the idea of getting rid of your PC will become much more attractive. At that point, each of us will have access to virtually unlimited online storage as well as a rich array of software services.... Having our files locked into our PC's hard drive will be an unnecessary nuisance.[78]

The concept of thin client access to the cloud may also alleviate the question of platform accessibility. Users may be able to access information regardless of their personal choice of operating system. And the current appeal of online gaming demonstrates that users on a variety of platforms can access Web 2.0 applications regardless of their operating system.

Web 2.0 Gaming

The world of online gaming attracts users from all over the world. Willy Reese is fourteen and lives outside of Richmond, Virginia. The soft-spoken teen enjoys football and archery, as well as a variety of computer games. His favorite is Infinity Ward's Call of Duty: Modern Warfare 2. He sometimes plays the first-person-shooter game by himself, sometimes online with other gamers, and sometimes with four or five friends from school. "We don't plan when to play, we just know when everyone is going to be on,"[79] he says. He uses the Sony PlayStation 3, as do his friends. Although the game is available for other gaming consoles, such as Microsoft's Xbox 360, if one of his friends had an Xbox and installed the game, he would be unable to join the group for online play, because the PlayStation and Xbox systems are incompatible.

However, the future of gaming may be tied to the evolving state of Web 2.0, where games played through Web 2.0 sites are increasingly popular. Men and women of all ages have discovered that there are games on the Internet that appeal to their tastes and that can be played no matter what system they use. For example, a retired U.S. government technology specialist in North Carolina plays Café World on Facebook with a personal computer, while a publishing media specialist in Massachusetts plays it on a Macintosh computer. What enables them to play the same game on different operating systems is that Café World was developed with the Internet in mind. Zynga Game Network, Inc., the company that developed Café World and other popular online games, uses the API from Facebook and other social networks in order to create games that are compatible no matter what operating system the user has.

The challenge for game developers and Web 2.0 site administrators for the years to come is to ensure that the gamers are using age-appropriate programs. Games bought at stores and downloaded for consoles have a ratings system. Currently there are no ratings for games found on Facebook, so users can play any of the games that are available as long as they say they are old enough to have an account (minimum age is fourteen). However, there is currently no means for verifying each person's age.

The questions of age appropriateness and verification remain to be solved. Because Internet access seems to be everywhere, many individuals and groups express concerns about keeping young users safe and their information secure when they go online. Others raise questions about the appropriateness of providing access to the Web to young people of any age.

Web 2.0 at School

Undoubtedly the Internet has helped revolutionize how young people access information. Countless schools have computers for student use, designed for accessing information and for completing assignments. But as students become more adept with technology, school administrators, parents, and educators debate how to ensure that the school computers are used appropriately.

Educators often network with colleagues to discuss ideas. Many do this by joining a social networking site. Classroom 2.0 is a social network for anyone interested in social media and

Web 2.0 in education. The site has attracted educators from all over the world, who post questions and share success stories on the site's discussion boards.

Many success stories include student-directed blogs or collaborative Web sites called wikis, to which the students can add their own creative efforts in writing, art, video, or music. The students integrate information from such Web 2.0 news aggregator sites as Digg or Delicious with images of copyright-free photos from sites such as Flickr or FreeStockPhotos.com to complete their assignments. Web 2.0 technologies also enable them to collaborate with students hundreds or thousands of miles away, through blog posts, wikis, or even video chats. For example, the World History and Current Events class at West Forsyth High School in Atlanta, Georgia, uses the video chat feature of Skype to interact with students from Russia, France, and Brazil. Some educators join networks such as Moodle or Edmodo, where they can post assignments and to which students can upload their completed work.

Web 2.0 has changed the way students use computers at school and how they access information from the Internet.

A Fifth Grader Looks Forward

Ally Jones lives in Virginia. The vivacious eleven-year-old enjoys art and writing in her journal, and playing a variety of online games. Her favorite is Disney's Pirates of the Caribbean, saying, "Usually when I finish my homework, I go straight to 'Pirates.' It's the most fun ever. They even sent me an email asking for my opinions about the game!"

Ally has a number of opinions about the game; her mother says she's working on a letter back to Disney that is now over four pages long. And she has a number of ideas about the future of the Web. She envisions increased safety for kids and computers small enough "to fit in your pocket," and thinks it would be better if computers could be voice activated, "so you wouldn't have to type."

Although she feels that searching the Web will become easier with time, she also feels that more aspects of the Web will cost money. "I think people will get greedy over the Web by charging a lot of money just to print stuff or play one simple game."

Ally Jones, interview with the author, February 10, 2010.

As technology continues to advance and new devices are introduced, educators wonder how these new tools will fit into the classrooms of the future. Following the introduction of Apple's iPad tablet computer in spring 2010, a discussion on Classroom 2.0's forums imagined the possibilities of iPads replacing laptops in classrooms. Some educators believe that few school districts could afford to outfit classrooms with the devices; others mention that security parameters and controls would need to be developed by parents, educators, and administrators first. The key to integrating any devices that can access Web 2.0 sites will be to ensure the students' safety while they learn and to ensure that their information remains secure from prying eyes both inside and outside the network.

Is Anyone Anonymous on the Web?

As the Internet has grown, so have concerns about privacy. Even before the advent of Web 2.0, companies such as Internet service providers and retail outlets collected

data about Internet users. This data included passwords, login names, screen names, surfing histories, and credit card information in order to combat credit card fraud and identity theft. With Web 2.0 social networks and search engines collect users' profiles in order to display ads for goods and services tailored to the individual. Additionally governments collect information in order to track such illegal pursuits such as drug trafficking, Internet hacking, and terrorist activity.

The entities collecting the data, and the amount of data collected, prompt some observers to wonder if it is possible for Internet users to remain anonymous when online. In December 2009 and January 2010, the Pew Internet & American Life Project conducted a survey that asked nearly nine hundred international technology experts and critics for their views about what may happen to the Internet between 2010 and 2020. One of the topics was the future of anonymity. In the view of many respondents, online anonymity is and will continue to be challenged in the coming years. Some wrote that new methods to provide identity authentication would become widespread. Others felt that new laws and regulations will strengthen confidentiality and anonymity.

For Stephen Downes of Canada's National Research Council, both confidentiality and security will remain the choice and responsibility of the Internet user. He says:

> Opportunities, technologies, and legal license will continue to protect anonymity. . . . However, many people will in most circumstances elect to assert their identity in order to protect their own interests. Online banking, personal websites and social networks, etc., require that a person protect his or her identity. Where authentication is voluntary, and clearly in the client's interests, and nonpervasive, people will gladly accept the restraints. Just as they accept the constraint of using keys to lock the car and house door but have the prerogative to, if they wish, leave either unlocked.[80]

Other respondents mentioned that there may be a middle ground between what is public on the Web and what is private. The term that identifies this middle ground is *pseudonymity.*

Locked, Unlocked, or Partially Locked

The respondents of the Pew survey also brought up concerns of partial privacy. Some of them believed that the key to the future of the Web is pseudonymity, in which an Internet user provides small pieces of authenticated information. Marcel Bullinga, a futurist at FutureCheck, defines pseudonymity as "I stay anonymous, but I hand out a trusted and checked piece of information, stating . . . that I am a male, or that I am under 18, or both."[81] Many felt that pseudonymity would enable users to continue to contribute to blogs or comment on news stories without loss of security or confidentiality.

Pseudonymity may also become the key to accessing information on the Web of the future. Future security developers may construct sites with varying levels of security that include pseudonymity. For example, a U.S. government Web site could provide free and open access to information about public lands and names of elected officials without any need for authentication. A second level, requiring pseudnonymous authentication, could provide an employee access to his or her e-mail and personal files, and a third level, requiring a retina scan, could provide access to secure government information such as employee records. The varying levels would ensure that only certain individuals would have access to certain information. In this scenario, a journalist would have access to government press releases and names of individuals to contact for stories but would not have legal access to those employees' personal files.

"Cover What You Do Best, Link to the Rest"

The proliferation of Web 2.0 services and sites has changed the landscape of the Internet experience. Citizen journalism, on-the-spot photography, and microblogging that can literally save lives have led to a change in how news is defined, and each challenges the traditional media's ability to cover events around the world.

The changes led Jeff Jarvis, director of the interactive journalism program at the City University of New York's Graduate School of Journalism, to reexamine how journalists should cover news. In a February 2007 blog post, he created what he called "a new rule for newspapers: Cover what you do best. Link to the rest."[82] Since that time, the slogan has been taken up newspapers and Web 2.0 media contributors. One journalist, Scott Lewis of voiceofsandiego .org, a nonprofit news organization in California, espoused it in a Twitter exchange with a local colleague. When David Rolland, editor of *San Diego CityBeat,* an alternative newspaper, tweeted, "We both cover news in San Diego. We compete for stories,"[83] Lewis replied, "I don't see it that way. We do what we do best & link to rest. Stories aren't owned, they just tell part of the big picture."[84]

The "big picture" depends on one's perspective. To the staff on a student newspaper, the big picture may be the budget cuts that will lead to the elimination of the Music

Department, or why a popular teacher is retiring. To a local newspaper or blogger, it may be why unemployment has risen or why a highway bridge collapsed. To others, it is the future of national and international affairs. And, to other observers, it is the future of the entire Internet.

Next Generation of Internet

In his 1999 book *Weaving the Web,* World Wide Web inventor Tim Berners-Lee shares his vision for the future of the Internet. He writes that he envisions a time when

> machines become capable of analyzing all the data on the Web—the content, links, and transactions between people and computers. A "Semantic Web," which should make this possible, has yet to emerge, but when it does, the day-to-day mechanisms of trade, bureaucracy, and our daily lives will be handled by machines talking to machines, leaving humans to provide the inspiration and intuition. . . . Once [this dream] is reached, the Web will be a place where the whim of a human being and the reasoning of a machine will coexist in an ideal, powerful mixture.[85]

More than a decade after Berners-Lee's book was published, technology experts believe that his vision will form a large

China's new long-distance "e-bus" is similar to Empire High School's Internet Bus. However, the e-bus has only ten seats, each of them is equipped with a computer so that passengers can surf the Internet for free during their ride.

part of the next generation of the Internet experience, called Web 3.0.

Some observers believe that Web 3.0 will combine the best features of Web 2.0, such as interactivity and localized search results, with the new technologies envisioned by Berners-Lee. The Semantic Web would enable search engines to understand the context of a search, based on a user's profile, which could include information based on the user's hobbies, memberships in social networks, groups and organizations, as well as recommendations from friends or consumer groups. For example, a search for "mustangs" today returns results for both wild horses and Ford automobiles; a Semantic Web search for "mustangs" by an automobile collector would filter out the results related to horses.

The shift from Web 2.0 to 3.0 may be subtle and perceived best in hindsight. For example, future historians may note that a pioneering effort in the Vail School District in Arizona is an example of the shift. In the fall of 2009, the district outfitted one of its Empire High School buses with a wireless Internet router. In the *New York Times* Sam Dillon writes,

> The students call it the Internet Bus, and what began as a high-tech experiment has had an old-fashioned—and unexpected—result. Wi-Fi access has transformed what was often a boisterous bus ride into a rolling study hall, and behavioral problems have virtually disappeared. "It's made a big difference," said J.J. Johnson, the bus's driver. "Boys aren't hitting each other, girls are busy, and there's not so much jumping around."[86]

The bus's route winds through mountain roads and takes over an hour in each direction. Students now use the trip to research and polish homework assignments and e-mail them to their teachers.

While the Internet Bus may be a Web 3.0 experience that is not too far removed from Web 2.0, other forward-looking technology enthusiasts envision Web 3.0 as offering an experience that is quantum leaps ahead of today. Some visions involve wearable devices that provide constant connections to the Internet through eye-activated menus, or a three-dimensional holographic experience similar to today's virtual worlds games, where users can walk and interact with other visitors.

Such ideas lead some technology observers to question the direction in which the Web is evolving. Some believe that the Internet continues to grow in the same way as Tim Berners-Lee envisioned it—without any one company, government, or network exerting control. Others are not so sure.

"Do the Right Thing"

Technology and media observer Tim O'Reilly is concerned about the direction that the Web may be taking. He has been involved with the Internet since the early 1990s and is responsible for popularizing the term *Web 2.0*. His company sponsors annual Web 2.0 conferences to examine emerging online developments and technologies. In a speech at the 2009 event in New York City, he expressed concerns about what he saw as a troubling trend. He pointed to the iPhone Apple Store and its exclusive line of applications, saying that Apple's policies are contrary to the open nature of the Web. He said, "It's not an open system in the same way the Web was. Apple decides who gets to put an application up, what does that application do, when does it infringe on Apple's business. This isn't the way the Web works."[87]

He also cited Google's innovative turn-by-turn directions feature, which has voice activation and recognition, but which is only available through Android-run phones. Although Google was meshing a number of technologies the company had developed, he pointed out that Google was also acting like Apple in making it exclusively available on Android phones.

O'Reilly likened these situations to a concept from J.R.R. Tolkien's fantasy series, The Lord of the Rings. In the books, there is one ring of power that controls all the other rings, and it bends the will of anyone who possesses it to its bidding. According to O'Reilly, the model of the Web, until now, has been that everyone used bits and pieces from other people to develop their services, and he now wonders if the situation is changing. He said, "Is it contributing to the openness of the Web, or is it leading us down the path where one provider says, 'You must work with me across all of your applications. My one ring is the ring that controls all.'"[88]

With that in mind, O'Reilly encouraged the Web aficionados and developers in the audience to work to keep the Web open by building on the bits and pieces of others. He reiterated the words of Jeff Jarvis—"Do what you do best, and link to the rest"—as worthwhile advice. But he also exhorted them to follow the words of legendary American novelist, critic, and essayist Mark Twain: "Do the right thing. You will gratify some people, and astonish the rest."

NOTES

Introduction: An Eighth Grader and the World Wide Web

1. Heather Coken, interview with author, January 10, 2010.
2. Coken, interview with author.
3. Coken, interview with author.
4. Coken, interview with author.

Chapter 1: Web 1.0 Evolves into Web 2.0

5. Leonard Kleinrock, correspondence with author, June 29, 2010.
6. Janet Abbate, *Inventing the Internet*, Cambridge MA: MIT Press, 1999, p. 106.
7. Ray Tomlinson, "The First Network Email," OpenMap (Web site), http://openmap.bbn.com/~tomlinso/ray/firstemailframe.html.
8. Quoted in Robert Mackey, "Internet Star @ Least 473 Years Old," *New York Times News*, May 4, 2009, http://thelede.blogs.nytimes.com/2009/05/04/internet-star-least-473-years-old.
9. Quoted in Mackey, "Internet Star @ Least 473 Years Old."
10. Quoted in Abbate, *Inventing the Internet*, p. 107.
11. Quoted in Judy O'Neill, "An Interview with Vinton Cerf," research paper, Minneapolis, MN: Charles Babbage Institute, April 24, 1990, www.cbi.umn.edu/oh/pdf.phtml?id=81.
12. Tim Berners-Lee with Mark Fischetti, *Weaving the Web: The Original Design and Ultimate Destiny of the World Wide Web by Its Inventor,* New York: HarperCollins, 1999, pp. 33–34.
13. Berners-Lee, *Weaving the Web,* p. 38.
14. Berners-Lee, *Weaving the Web,* p. 51.
15. Gary Wolfe, "The (Second Phase of the) Revolution Has Begun," *Wired,* October 1994. Available at http://www.wired.com/wired/archive/2.10/mosaic.html.
16. Berners-Lee, *Weaving the Web,* p. 36.
17. Gary Rivlin, "A Retail Revolution Turns 10," *New York Times,* July 10, 2005, www.nytimes.com/2005/07/10/business/yourmoney/10amazon.html?_r=1.
18. Karl Taro Greenfeld, "Meet the Napster," *Time,* October 2, 2000. Available at http://www.time.com/time/magazine/article/0,9171,998068-2,00.html.
19. Ward Cunningham, "What Is Wiki," June 27, 2002, www.wiki.org/wiki.cgi?WhatIsWiki.

20. Darcy DiNucci, "Fragmented Future," *Print*, July 1999. Available at http://www.cole20.com/web-20-history-fragmented-future-recovered/.

Chapter 2:
The New News

21. Quoted in Donna Bogatin, "Digg: Kevin Rose Talks 'The Real Deal' in Exclusive Interview," ZDNet, September 15, 2006, http://blogs.zdnet.com/micro-markets/index.php?p=446.
22. Joseph Thornley, "What Is 'Social Media'?" Pro PR (Web site), April 8, 2008, http://propr.ca/2008/what-is-social-media.
23. Quoted in David Sarno, "Twitter Creator Jack Dorsey Illuminates the Site's Founding Document, Part I," *Los Angeles Times*, February 18, 2009, http://latimesblogs.latimes.com/technology/2009/02/twitter-creator.html.
24. Jack Dorsey, "Just Setting up My Twttr," March 21, 2006, http://twitter.com/jack/status/.
25. Leigh Mills, "Idk! lol but ily 2 death . . . WHAT?!?," *NBC15 Blog*, July 14, 2009. Available at http://www.nbc15.com/blogs/leighmills/50801387.html.
26. Quoted in Martha Irvine, "Is blogging a Slog? Some Young People Think So," Associated Press, February 3, 2010, http://abcnews.go.com/Technology/wirestory?id=9740344&page=2.
27. Andrew Lennon, "A Conversation with Twitter Co-Founder Jack Dorsey," The Daily Anchor (Web site), February 12, 2009, www.thedailyanchor.com/2009/02/12/a-conversation-with-twitter-co-founder-jack-dorsey.
28. Stephanie Busari, "Tweeting the Terror: How Social Media Reacted to Mumbai," CNN.com, November 28, 2008, http://edition.cnn.com/2008/WORLD/asiapcf/11/27/mumbai.twitter/index.html.
29. Quoted in Lennon, "A Conversation with Twitter Co-Founder Jack Dorsey."
30. Busari, "Tweeting the Terror."
31. Pear Analytics, "Twitter Study—August 2009," Pear Analytics, August 12, 2009, http://www.pearanalytics.com/blog/wp-content/uploads/2010/05/Twitter-Study-August-2009.pdf.
32. Christi Day, "Southwest Airlines Underscores Customer of Size Policy," Southwest Airlines "Nuts About Southwest" blog, February 14, 2010. Available at http://www.blogsouthwest.com/blog/not-so-silent-bob?page=3.
33. Quoted in CNN.com, "Oprah, Ashton Kutcher Mark Twitter 'Turning Point,'" CNN.com, April 18, 2009, www.cnn.com/2009/TECH/04/17/ashton.cnn.twitter.battle.
34. Mike Laurie, "How Social Media Has Changed Us," Mashable (Web site), January 7, 2010, http://mashable.com/2010/01/07/social-media-changed-us.

Chapter 3:
Social Networks

35. Quoted in Gary Rivlin, "Wallflower at the Web Party," *New York Times*, October 15, 2006, www.nytimes.com/2006/10/15/business/yourmoney/15friend.html.

36. Rivlin, "Wallflower at the Web Party."

37. Quoted in Claire Hoffman, "The Battle for Facebook," *Rolling Stone*, June 26, 2008. Available at http://web.archive.org/web/20080703201450/www.rollingstone.com/news/story/21129674/the_battle_for_facebook/print.

38. Hoffman, "The Battle for Facebook."

39. Quoted in Hoffman, "The Battle for Facebook."

40. Ben Gold, "Facebook Hammers MySpace on Almost All Key Features," Mashable, June 10, 2007, http://mashable.com/2007/06/10/facebook-hammers-myspace-on-almost-all-key-features.

41. Clay D. Hysell, interview with author, February 17, 2010.

42. Hysell, interview with author.

43. Hysell, interview with author.

44. Quoted in Chris Baylor, "Using Social Media for More than Just Status Updates," WEAU.com, February 17, 2010, www.weau.com/news/headlines/84633272.html.

45. BBC News, "Colombians in Huge Farc Protest," BBC News, February 4, 2008, http://news.bbc.co.uk/2/hi/americas/7225824.stm.

46. Jose Antonio Vargas, "Obama Raised Half a Billion Online," *Washington Post*, November 20, 2008, http://voices.washingtonpost.com/44/2008/11/obama-raised-half-a-billion-on.html.

47. U.S. Department of the Navy, "Performance Work Statement for Social Networking and Community Development," January 28, 2010, https://www.fbo.gov/download/c1d/c1d563a0bc7010776f5eefc1bda48a83/PWS_for_Social_Networking_and_Community_Development.doc.

48. Amber Corrin, "MilBook (Securely) Harnesses Social Media Behind DOD Firewalls," *Defense Systems*, January 21, 2010, http://defensesystems.com/articles/2010/01/20/milbook-military-social-media.aspx.

49. Quoted in Corrin, "MilBook (Securely) Harnesses Social Media Behind DOD Firewalls."

50. Yosemite National Park, Twitter feed, January 29, 2010, http://twitter.com/YosemiteNPS.

51. Kari Cobb, interview with author, February 22, 2010.

52. Robert McMillan, "Researchers: Web 2.0 Security Seriously Flawed," *PCWorld*, April 25, 2007, www.pcworld.com/article/131215/researchers_web_20_security_seriously_flawed.html.

53. Kevin Cullen, "The Untouchable Mean Girls," *Boston Globe*, January 24, 2010, www.boston.com/community/moms/articles/2010/01/24/the_untouchable_mean_girls.

54. Quoted in Martin Finucane, "S. Hadley School Officials Take Action Against Students in Bullying Case," *Boston Globe*, February 23, 2010, www.boston.com/news/local/breaking_news/2010/02/s_hadley_school.html.

55. Amy Jones, correspondence with author, February 17, 2010.

Chapter 4: Mashing, Memes, and More

56. Rev2.org, "YouTube—The Complete Profile," Rev2.org, October 2, 2006, www.rev2.org/2006/10/02/youtube-the-complete-profile.

57. John Cloud, "The Gurus of YouTube," *Time*, December 16, 2006. Available at http://www.time.com/time/magazine/article/0,9171,1570721,00.html.

58. James Niccolai, "So What Is an Enterprise Mashup, Anyway?" *PCWorld*, April 23, 2008, www.pcworld.com/businesscenter/article/145039/so_what_is_an_enterprise_mashup_anyway.html.

59. DJ Earworm, description of Maroon 5 mashup, 2010. Available at http://djearworm.com.

60. Quoted in Jo Piazza, "DJ Earworm: Man Behind Viral Year-End Mash-ups," CNN.com, January 25, 2010, www.cnn.com/2010/SHOWBIZ/Music/01/25/dj.earworm/index.html.

61. Quoted in Piazza, "DJ Earworm."

62. Richard Rushfield and Claire Hoffman, "Mystery Fuels Huge Popularity of Web's Lonelygirl15," *Los Angeles Times*, September 8, 2006, http://articles.latimes.com/2006/sep/08/entertainment/et-lonelygirl8.

63. Dave Carroll, interview by Chris Wragge, *Early Show*, CBS, July 10, 2009, www.youtube.com/watch?v=PGNtQF3n6VY.

64. Dave Carroll, "United Breaks Guitars: A Statement," YouTube video, July 10, 2009, www.youtube.com/watch?v=pl-_pDNS7Ik.

65. Warren Zenna and Max Rosen, "How To Make A Video Go Viral," Indigo Productions Video and Multimedia, June 17, 2009. Available at http://indigoprod.com/nyc-video-production-blog/2009/06/how-to-make-a-video-go-viral/.

66. Jennifer Van Grove, "Social Media Break: 5 Internet Memes to Make You LOL," Mashable, March 4, 2009, http://mashable.com/2009/03/04/funny-memes.

67. Dan Zarella and Alison Driscoll, "The Anatomy of a Facebook Meme," Mashable, April 3, 2009, http://mashable.com/2009/04/03/facebook-meme.

68. SurveyUSA, "You Wouldn't Get This from Any Other Pollster," Survey USA, April 9, 2008, www.surveyusa.com/index.php/2008/04/09/you-wouldnt-get-this-from-any-other-pollster.

69. Quoted in *Los Angeles Times*, "Web Scout Exclusive! Rick Astley, King of the 'Rickroll,' Talks About His Song's Second Coming," *Los Angeles Times*, March 25, 2008, http://latimesblogs

.latimes.com/webscout/2008/03/rick-astley-kin.html.

70. Quoted in Piazza, "DJ Earworm."

71. Piazza, "DJ Earworm."

72. Piazza, "DJ Earworm."

73. U.S. Copyright Office, "Fair Use," U.S. Copyright Office, May 2009, www.copyright.gov/fls/fl102.html.

Chapter 5: Beyond Web 2.0

74. Quoted in Peter Kafka, "Zuckerberg: Facebook Will Have a Business Plan in Three Years," *Business Insider,* October 9, 2008, www.businessinsider.com/2008/10/zuckerberg-facebook-will-have-a-business-plan-in-three-years.

75. Quentin Hardy and Evan Hessel, "GooTube," *Forbes,* June 18, 2008. Available at http://www.forbes.com/forbes/2008/0616/050.html.

76. Todd Wright, "Earthquake Survivor Calls iPhone a Life Saver," NBC Miami, January 20, 2010, www.nbcmiami.com/news/local-beat/Earthquake-Survivor-Says-iPhone-a-Life-Saver—82081602.html.

77. Chris Kanaracus, "Salesforce.com Sets Sights on the Smallest Businesses," *PCWorld,* September 1, 2009, www.pcworld.com/businesscenter/article/171285/salesforcecom_sets_sights_on_the_smallest_businesses.html

78. Nicholas Carr, *The Big Switch: Rewiring the World, from Edison to Google,* New York: Norton, 2008, pp. 80–81.

79. Willy Reese, interview with author, February 14, 2010.

80. Quoted in Janna Anderson and Lee Rainie, "Future of the Internet IV," Pew Internet & American Life Project, February 19, 2010, http://pewinternet.org/Reports/2010/Future-of-the-Internet-IV.aspx.

81. Quoted in Anderson and Rainie, "Future of the Internet IV."

82. Jeff Jarvis, "New Rule: Cover What You Do Best. Link to the Rest," BuzzMachine (Web site), February 22, 2007, www.buzzmachine.com/2007/02/22/new-rule-cover-what-you-do-best-link-to-the-rest.

83. David Rolland, Twitter feed, January 19, 2010, http://twitter.com/drolland.

84. Scott Lewis, Twitter feed, January 19, 2010, http://twitter.com/vosdscott.

85. Berners-Lee, *Weaving the Web,* pp. 157–58.

86. Sam Dillon, "Wi-Fi Turns Rowdy Bus Into Rolling Study Hall," *New York Times,* February 11, 2010.

87. Tim O'Reilly, "The War for the Web," keynote address, Web 2.0 Expo, New York, November 17, 2009, www.youtube.com/watch?v=EYRC8nfZ67M.

88. O'Reilly, "The War for the Web."

Advanced Research Projects Agency (ARPA): An agency created by the U.S. Department of Defense in 1958 to fund American scientific research.

application: In computer science, software that is designed to help the user perform a specific task. An application may be hosted on an individual's computer, such as a word processing program, or on a Web server, such as a media player.

application programming interface (API): A type of software that enables computer programs to communicate without user input.

ARPANET: Computer network created by ARPA funding; the forerunner of the Internet.

browser: A Web program that enables users to read information on the Internet.

CERN: Conseil Europeén pour La Rechereche Nucléaire (European Particle Physics Laboratory) located on the French-Swiss border in Geneva, Switzerland.

cross-scripting attack: A type of online attack that targets insecure Web sites, which results in the attacker being able to run unauthorized code on the victim's browser, resulting in loss of data such as login names and passwords.

cross-site request forgery: A type of online attack that tricks a Web site into believing that it is exchanging data with a user who is properly logged on, but who may actually have left the site without logging off, resulting in the attacker gaining access to privileged information on the user's computer.

exabyte: A unit of data measurement. One exabyte equals one thousand petabytes.

gateway: A device that enables data to flow between different networks.

graphic user interface (GUI): An interface for issuing commands to a computer using a pointing device, such as a mouse, that activates and changes graphical images on a monitor.

host: A computer connected to a network, such as the World Wide Web.

hypertext: Originally, a term for a document that includes links. Current usage includes other media as well as text documents.

Internet: Originally "inter-network," Internet refers to the interconnections of computers worldwide. Often synonymous with World Wide Web.

mashup: Term for a new creation that combines two or more features (such as video, data, or images) to create a new way of presenting information.

meme: An Internet image, phrase, or video that spreads rapidly among Web users.

packet: A unit into which information is divided for transmission across the Internet.

petabyte: A unit of data measurement. One petabyte equals 1 million gigabytes.

profile: Personal information, such as age, school, and hometown that is created by Web users when joining a social network or other site requiring membership.

protocol: A language and a set of rules that enable computers to interact in a well-defined way.

pseudonymity: Term for partial anonymity on the Internet, in which a user provides only selected portions of information for site authentication.

retweet: A Twitter message that is forwarded from earlier users.

Semantic Web: A projected version of the Web in which machines are able to analyze all the data on the Internet.

server: A computer that provides services to other computers across a network, such as within a school, a company, or the Internet.

thin client: A type of computer with limited capabilities and software that is designed to connect to the Internet in order to run programs online.

traditional media: Collective term that refers to any or all of the pre-Internet forms of media, including radio, television, and newspapers.

transmission control protocol/Internet protocol (TCP/IP): The technical term for the operations that allow computers to connect to and receive information from the Internet.

tweet: A message sent on the microblog service Twitter.

viral: A story, image, or video that spreads extremely quickly among Web users.

virus: A small computer program that is spread from machine to machine, often by e-mail, that may harm the computer's operating system or the user's ability to perform tasks.

voice over Internet protocol (VoIP): A technology that enables computer users to make telephone calls, hold video chats, and to send text messages via Internet connections.

wiki: A Web site that allows easy editing or collaborative effort.

World Wide Web: Term coined by Tim Berners-Lee in 1990 to describe the set of all information accessible using computers and networking. Often abbreviated as "the Web."

yottabyte: A unit of data measurement. One yottabyte equals one thousand zettabytes.

zettabyte: A unit of data measurement. One zettabyte equals 1 million petabytes.

FOR MORE INFORMATION

Books

Tim Berners-Lee with Mark Fischetti, *Weaving the Web: The Original Design and Ultimate Destiny of the World Wide Web by Its Inventor.* New York: HarperCollins, 1999. Berners-Lee shares his inspiration behind the Web, as well as his personal accomplishments in the years since its arrival.

Terry Burrows, *Blogs, Wikis, MySpace and More: Everything You Wanted to Know About Using Web 2.0 but Are Afraid to Ask.* Chicago, IL: Chicago Review Press, 2008. This is a handy guide to a variety of Web 2.0 services, sites, and trends, along with techniques for sharing videos, writing blogs, and more.

Nicholas Carr, *The Big Switch: Rewiring the World, from Edison to Google.* New York: Norton, 2008. This book uses fascinating stories from history, including the development of the electricity industry, to propose that access to the Internet will eventually become a utility, in the same way that electricity is today.

T. Brian Chatfield, *The MySpace.com Handbook: The Complete Guide for Members and Parents.* Ocala FL: Atlantic, 2008. This book provides valuable information on how to set up a MySpace account safely and securely and offers parents tips on effective Internet security and dealing with potential online threats.

Katie Hafner and Matthew Lyon, *Where Wizards Stay Up Late: The Origins of the Internet.* New York: Simon & Schuster, 1998. This book discusses the origins of the ARPANET, concentrating on the individuals who created it, along with their personalities, their eccentricities, their conflicts, and their collaborations.

Todd Kelsey, *Social Networking Spaces: From Facebook to Twitter and Everything in Between.* New York: Apress, 2010. This book's easily accessible format explores how to use a variety of social networks to their fullest, including how to use them with mobile devices.

Laura Lambert, Hilary W. Poole, Chris Woodford, and Christo J.P. Moschovitis, eds., *The Internet: A Historical Encyclopedia.* Santa Barbara, CA: ABC-CLIO, 2005. This three-volume set provides biographical profiles of important Internet figures (vol. 1), issues and controversies (vol. 2), and an Internet chronology (vol. 3). Biographies include World Wide Web founder Tim Berners-Lee, TCP/IP developers Robert Kahn and Vinton Cerf, and many others.

Tim O'Reilly and Sarah Milstein, *The Twitter Book*. Sebastopol, CA: O'Reilly Media, 2009. Using screenshots of tweets and Twitter applications, this book illustrates how to get the most out of Twitter.

Leah Pearlman and Carolyn Abram, *Facebook for Dummies*. 2nd ed. Hoboken, NJ: Wiley, 2009. In this second edition, the authors present updated information on how to create a profile on Facebook, how to keep information secure, how to upload photos, how to create a fan page or a group, and much more.

Nancy E. Willard, *Cyber-Safe Kids, Cyber-Savvy Teens: Helping Young People Learn to Use the Internet Safely and Responsibly*. Hoboken NJ: Wiley, 2007. This book offers advice on how to keep people of any age safe on the Web.

Internet Sources

David Berlind, "What Is a Mashup?" video presentation, ZDNet, February 6, 2006, http://news.zdnet.com/2422-13569_22-152729.html.

Pete Cashmore, "Southwest Tweets, Blogs Apology to Kevin Smith," Mashable, February 14, 2010, http://mashable.com/2010/02/14/southwest-kevin-smith.

CNN.com, "Survivors Pray for the Aftershocks to Stop," January 13, 2010, www.cnn.com/2010/WORLD/americas/01/13/haiti.victims.

Larry Magid, "Social Networking Belongs in School," CNET, February 25, 2010, http://news.cnet.com/8301-19518_3-10459983-238.html.

National Crime Prevention Council, "Cyberbullying FAQ for Teens," www.ncpc.org/topics/cyberbullying/cyberbullying-faq-for-teens.

Judy O'Neill, "An Interview with Vinton Cerf," research paper, Minneapolis, MN: Charles Babbage Institute, April 24, 1990, www.cbi.umn.edu/oh/pdf.phtml?id=81.

U.S. Copyright Office, "Fair Use," May 2009, www.copyright.gov/fls/fl102.html.

John D. Varlaro, "Tweetiquette for Beginners," The Humanist Strategist, April 20, 2009, www.thehumanisticstrategist.com/articles/2009/4/20/tweetiquette-for-beginners.html.

Todd Wright, "Earthquake Survivor Calls iPhone a Life Saver," NBC Miami, January 20, 2010, www.nbcmiami.com/news/local-beat/Earthquake-Survivor-Says-iPhone-a-Life-Saver--82081602.html

Periodicals

John Cloud, "The Gurus of YouTube," *Time*, December 16, 2006.

Sam Dillon, "Wi-Fi Turns Rowdy Bus Into Rolling Study Hall," *New York Times,* February 11, 2010.

Karl Taro Greenfeld, "Meet the Napster," *Time,* October 2, 2000.

Quentin Hardy and Evan Hessel, "GooTube," *Forbes,* June 18, 2008.

Claire Hoffman, "The Battle for Facebook," *Rolling Stone,* June 26, 2008.

Robert Mackey, "Internet Star @Least 473 Years Old," *New York Times,* May 4, 2009.

Gary Rivlin, "A Retail Revolution Turns 10," *New York Times,* July 10, 2005.

Gary Rivlin, "Wallflower at the Web Party," *New York Times,* October 15, 2006.

Gary Wolfe, "The (Second Phase of the) Revolution Has Begun," *Wired,* October 1994.

Web Sites

Earworm Mashups (http://djearworm.com). This is the Web site of DJ Earworm, who shares insights and multimedia samples of his mashups.

Mashable (www.mashable.com). This site offers a wide range of issues related to social media, including memes, social networks, technology news, and more.

Rocketboom: Daily Internet Culture (www.rocketboom.com). This site provides a variety of humorous yet insightful videos from the Rocketboom Institute for Internet Studies, including several devoted to understanding memes (available in the "know your meme" category).

INDEX

PICTURE CREDITS

ABOUT THE AUTHOR

Andrew A. Kling worked as a National Park Service ranger in locations across the United States for over fifteen years. He now works as a writer and editor for a variety of nonprofit organizations and as an interpretive media developer and consultant. He enjoys hockey, technology, studying flags, and spending time with his wife and their Norwegian forest cat, Chester.